Book Signing

Glenda Kemp-Harper

Glenda Kemp

Snake Dancer

Glenda Kemp-Harper

Published by Glenda Kemp-Harper
http://glendakemp.wordpress.com/

Cover design and formatting of photographs:
Clive Thompson
www.getclive.com

Copy editing and layout:
Anne Erikson
www.pagesave.org

ISBN-13: 978-1481244046
ISBN-10: 1481244043

Dedication

I dedicate this book to my four sisters because we shared the same womb, were hit by the same shrapnel and we each learnt to run a marathon with missing limbs.

And to all my sisters in Christ, because we share the same Father and are one in Christ. We run, not with uncertainty, the same race, to obtain an imperishable crown where we will be with Jesus forever and ever.

To my brother, Dale. A celebration of the thread of love that has woven its way into our lives and bound us together throughout all these years. I am so glad you are my brother.

And to my dearest child Kim, who is my inspiration and the most precious gift from God.

And finally, to my soulmate, Eliza. Because we are one in spirit, the Lord is doubly glorified in all we do. I thank you for always being there for me and for allowing me to be myself.

Tribute

Val Waldeck

You pulled me into your writers' convention and pushed me off into the deep end with such encouragement that I swam around in words of my past and present until the inside-out version reached the finishing line in perfect timing. And then you polished it off with your professional touch. I say thank you.

Val Ludik

Almost as if this book were a knitted garment, Val Ludik checked the unconnected sections and picked up the lost stitches and made it recognizable as a garment-to-be.

Anne Erikson

It was Anne who stitched everything together, threw out the ruffled snippets and sewed it together into a flawless garment which enchants the readers as she lures them in to Cinderella's Ball. When Val Waldeck said: 'I know an excellent editor,' she meant just that! This editor, Anne Erikson, honoured me with her presence at my house as she took the time to meet me in person. This beautiful lady oozed all the organization and order that was so lacking in my set-up. My sincere thanks and gratitude to Anne.

Clive Thompson

A big thank-you to Clive Thompson for using his creative gifts to design a cover that shows the bondage and freedom that is described in the book. And for reformatting the photos, making it possible for Anne to kindly slot them into place.

Contents

O Lord, I am your servant;

Yes, I am your servant, born into your household;

You have freed me from my chains.

I will offer you a sacrifice of thanksgiving

And call on the name of the Lord.

— Psalm 116:16–17

Prologue

'Heads' or 'Tails'?

There are two sides to this story of my life, in the same way as there are two sides to a coin.

I flipped the coin of my life over at the age of 15. I dropped it at the age of 21. I retrieved it when I was 47 and called out 'heads'.

So the first side of the story is one of shame and doom, telling of the time in my life when I lived in apparent freedom from obedience to the law, with the truth whispering all the time in the background — 'slaves to sin'. What a side to the coin! '… and what was the result? You are now ashamed of the things you used to do, things that end in eternal doom' (Romans 6:20–21).

The reason the world sat up and took notice was not because of what the Word said but because of a scandalous young woman who removed all her clothes and draped herself with a snake.

Then the flip side toppled that life of headlines, fame and comfort and zoomed me in to all the excitement and challenges that mature you into the person whom God intended you to be.

But that is not where I am going to begin.

Although I am now a new person in Jesus Christ, I will look back and start at the beginning. One big difference though, is that this time I have put my hand in the hand of the Man who stilled the waters.

1

The first years

Cape Town (1949-1955)

Some imaginary photos have to be stuck in front of your eyes as they show something that is to happen later. There is a picture in the photo album of me standing on a chair so I can reach the record player. Music was my mother's babysitter as she could leave me and come back hours later and find me still lost in sound.

Here is a picture of me 'saying a recitation'. I won a brooch for this. Then there was the Grade 1 concert. I can let you touch the smooth fabric of my 'Jingle Bells' dress with the cotton wool around the hem and the bells I shook.

It is so real in my memory that it scares me. Is this where a 'star' was born? See me with little ducks, cats and dogs and lazing in hot baths with four other sisters. There was also Christmas which was about wonderful gifts once a year. But all of this will not withstand the fire at Judgement Day.

Now I see one thing illuminated: I am on my knees talking to God the Father; speaking words that withstand the fire of hell:

'Ek is 'n kindjie klein. Liewe Jesus, maak my hartjie rein. Laat nicmand anders in my hartjie woon nie; net liewe Jesus alleen. Amen.'

English: 'I am a little child. Dear Jesus make my heart pure. Let nobody else live in my heart; just you alone, dear Jesus. Amen.'

Johannesburg (1955)

This happy life came to an end on the train trip from Cape Town to Johannesburg when my father was transferred. This trip is not without its memories. A mother cat and her litter we took with us on the journey would soon have been Jo'burg animals, had they not been discovered by the conductor doing his ticket rounds on the journey.

Joan (my next-eldest sister) and I were fooling around with my Christmas doll. Joan was dangling the doll with her one hand outside the train window in an effort to upset me. The next minute the doll was not in her hand any longer and the train was moving on. There was a hushed silence. I think I had to console her more than she did me, as we both grieved the unfortunate loss of a once-in-a-lifetime doll. I love my sisters dearly. Joan and I still had a long walk together ahead of us. The loss of that doll was only a hint of the terrible sadness that awaited us in Johannesburg.

* * * * *

When we lived in the Railway house in Maraisburg I learnt to ride a bike. It was my older brother's bike and I had to ride with my one leg through the frame. Wow, the thrill and forgotten skinned knees when I first balanced and stopped without falling off.

I held my first circus at that time. For days or maybe months I was the circus star who performed endless tricks. I think you would have been lucky to find me the right way up at that time as I was forever on my hands.

We went to Sunday School. I was terrified of not knowing the scripture verses we had to learn. If only I had known how eternally valuable those verses would be. Then my mother shouted at the minister because he came to our house for money and she was in need of money herself. End of Sunday School!

It was then that I became aware of the darker side that was creeping into our household. There were arguments. One night my mother and sisters were hiding in the bedroom because my father was angry and shouting. I think he was drunk. He was very angry. Then he demanded that I be given to him. He took me and kept me in the bedroom with him. I was scared but he did nothing to me.

I have only two other memories of my father. One was his anger at the dinner table. We kids were not allowed to talk and if we displayed bad table manners he would whack our fingers with the back of his knife. I don't think he ever hurt us. The other memory I have was of walking behind him and loving the sound his feet made when he walked, so I walked in his footsteps, wanting that sound to be repeated.

Life with my mother and stepfather (1956-1962)

And then there was no father and no sisters and no life. This was hell! Don't ask me how the transition happened as there is a blackout in my memory between one phase and the next. The facts are that my mother met a man, fell in love, became pregnant, left all of us, moved in with this man and married him, thus making him my stepfather.

Now I was living in an L-shaped bachelor flat in a block called Hermahoff, in La Rochelle, Johannesburg, with my working mother, my stepfather and a new baby brother. Joan (second youngest in the family) and Dirk (fourth eldest), were in an orphanage in Potchefstroom; Jean (third in line), was in a reformatory. Hermie (second eldest sister), quickly got married to escape the furnace and Linda (eldest sister) — lucky fish — was already married and out of the house.

The 'new' husband had said my mother could bring me along as I was the pretty little baby girl. Dear God, I wish you had intervened at this stage and taken me to the orphanage too. You did, however, give me the gift of a vivid imagination and most days I drifted along as the main character in a princess story. But at night I could not push the reality aside. And later that reality tore the fantasy to shreds for moments until I could crawl out again and embrace the stray dogs in the neighbourhood whose licks comforted and showed love to me. Many dogs were tied up on chains at that time and I was their silver lining in a dark cloud.

Then there were books. I can still smell the library and the silence. I learnt how to swap places with the characters in the stories, which always ended with 'and they lived happily ever after'.

This was in fact the end of my schooling. Of course I was there only to occupy the seat as that was required by the law, but my brain wanted nothing to do with anything that was real. The reality of the nights with my mother screaming in torture — I later learnt it was her loud lovemaking — and nightmares about coalmen who skinned me alive, were all that I could bear. Even washing my face in cold water did not wash away the nightmare that would just continue as I lay down on the bed with my baby brother, Dale.

One day my wonderful sister Jean, who must then have been 13 or 14, turned up at the door. She had run away from the reformatory. We embraced. We played music loudly. We danced. Suddenly my stepfather was there. My mother was there. Then Jean was chased out of the house. I ran crying after her, shouting, 'Jean, don't go.' I fell. My knees bled. Jean disappeared. Or did Jean bleed and my knees disappeared? Father, God, Jesus, where were you?

Jean is dead now. Lord, you took me in the Spirit to her deathbed in the hospital in June 1999 and she repeated after me: 'Jesus, I accept you as my Lord and my Saviour. I believe you are the Son of God. I believe you died for my sins. I am yours.'

Then, Father, you gave me proof by directing me to the movie of a man called Ian McCormack called *Dead Man Walking*, (not the Sean Penn movie). You showed me that we can be converted in the Spirit. Lord, did you already see this ending that day? Did you hear my prayer? That young girl was raped in body and in soul. You showed mercy.

A healing revelation from God

Many years later, during the interview for the new movie of my life, I could not get myself to say that I had been sexually abused by my stepfather. I just could not get myself to say it. When I got to writing the book I avoided the topic for days.

Then it was the Easter weekend. I sat in church looking at the cross. I saw Jesus on the cross. Then I had a vision of me walking to the cross, climbing up, looking Jesus in the eye, then turning and placing my body over his so that I could hang there with Him. I could see through his eyes. I saw the crowd below crucifying Him. Then in the crowd I saw my stepfather. I heard Jesus say, 'Father, forgive them for they know not what they are doing.' I saw my stepfather with the love Jesus had for him. This love flowed over to me. I forgave my stepfather as I knew Jesus forgives me. I was set free. The tomb was empty. I could go back to that room where it happened. All that is left is the 'linen cloths' as in Jesus' empty tomb. In memory, I can walk back into the past as the daughter of a King.

> 'Yet now He has reconciled you to Himself through the death of Christ in his physical body. As a result, he has brought you into his own presence, and you are holy and blameless as you stand before him without a single fault' (Col 1:22).

We moved into a two-bedroomed, corrugated iron house almost across the road from where Hermahoff flats were — 5 West Lane, La Rochelle.

The first memory that comes to mind is of being abused by my stepfather and of the things he would make me do to him when my mother had left for work. Afterwards I would get dressed and he would drive me to school in the little Morris Minor car. I would walk into class a scarred child. A child with a horrible secret.

> *'Lord, my prayer is for all those men who molest children. You know the broken world they come from. You know the pain that caused them to inflict pain. Give them new hearts. Hear their prayers and heal them. As I truly forgive my stepfather, Jesus, so forgive and heal those who live today that need You! Those that are dead are dead. I pray for the victims. Tell them they can rise out of the past, a new person with You. You make everything new.'*

The molestation stopped the day I thought, in my ignorance, that I was pregnant. My sister Jean, who was pregnant at the time, came to visit us. She shared how she found out she was pregnant by liquid that came from her breasts. I discovered liquid coming from my just-developing breasts. Thank you God, for my sisters. Hermie was in a stable marriage and, wonder of wonders, had met Jesus. I wrote her a letter, telling her everything. Then all hell broke loose. My mother screamed at me, accusing me of being a dishonoured woman now. ('Jesus, she was also in shock. She also did not know what she was doing.') Then I learnt what it was like to live with someone who hates you. My stepfather never addressed me again. He would talk to my mother and refer to me as 'that thing'. He would say 'Tell "that thing" to go and buy bread,' or 'Tell "that thing" to clean her room.'

'Oh, Lord, if only he knew who I was. That You, mighty God, had Your Name written on my forehead. That I was the true daughter of a King. He would have fallen on his face in terror and fear of You. But he did not know. He did not know what he was doing.'

With Dale at the beachfront amusement park in Durban

Let's look at the bright side of things. The lovely park across the road. My precious little brother, Dale, who crawled deep into my heart. A big tree at the back of the house. Did I say tree? It was my horse, my den and meeting place with wonderful imaginary friends. The stray cat that became my inseparable shadow. Gigi, our big, fat, white rat that I refused to keep in a cage, so she lived with the regular rats under the wooden floor but always came when I called her. Once I bathed her and dried her with a green sack and she became our green rat, Gigi. And top of the animal list was Piet, my bearded dog. I think it is fair to say that Piet was the only one who ever showed any love towards me. My dog friends extended to whichever stray happened to be around. I know I fed the neighbour's dog that was permanently chained next door. At that stage I wanted to become a vet. Then there were the Saturday movies where we exchanged comics.

Movies! On my first day at high school the bus passed my school stop and I ended up in town. What the heck, I thought, I might as well go to the movies. I became such a regular in the cinema that they let me in for free. I must have seen Pollyanna a dozen times. I was going to be a movie star, come what may!

As for school; it just did not happen anymore. Later on I failed Standard 6 (Grade 8). How I passed any standard I don't know. I guess they only kept you in a standard for so long. I seriously did not even write anything in my books, if I had books. I never opened my school case.

Another happy moment was when my mother bought me a yellow hula hoop. Other than that, my mother disappeared out of my life. She was there but I did not think that she knew that I was there. She did not know or care if I had homework or not. She did not know if I went to school or not. I could sleep out with friends without asking or saying where I was, she could not care less. She was working and the new husband and baby were all that existed in her life. Once I ran away from home — but I hid on the front porch. After what seemed like days I came in again and no one noticed. This is when I vowed that I would not have a child if I could not be there for my child. I kept that promise and I always fetched my daughter from school and opened my home to her friends.

Yet I adored my mother more than anything. I remember arranging a surprise birthday party for her. I remember begging money from Jean's new husband to surprise my mother with linoleum for the kitchen floor. But my older brother came to visit and I gave him the money for a radio, so the floor never happened.

Joan also came to visit once a year. We both practically lived in the cinema. I used to drive her crazy as I was always acting and singing, whatever she said. She was there when I phoned Jamie Uys (a South African film producer) to say I wanted to be a movie star. He arranged for Joan and me to meet a then well-known Afrikaans actress, Miemsie Retief. We had our photo taken with her and printed in the newspaper. I had to borrow a dress from a friend for the occasion.

There are two incidents that shamed me and for which I have received total forgiveness from my heavenly Father. The first happened while living in the flat. There was a couple who owned a dairy around the corner. They took pity on me and allowed me to help in the dairy. They also opened their house to me and provided me with the only three dresses I had. Then one day I broke their trust. I was in Standard 2 (Grade 4). My teacher was a young lady who should not have been in teaching. She favoured whoever showered her with gifts. I also wanted to give her a gift. I wanted to be teacher's pet for that one day. If only I had a gift. That is what I saw when I looked at the dairy lady's jewellery box. A gift for my teacher. So I stole it — the whole box filled with a collection of jewellery accumulated over the years. The teacher took it. That day I could clean the board. I could stand next to the teacher. I was the pet.

> 'Lord, how I pray for every teacher in the world. How the world needs you, Jesus. Thank You for forgiving me. Forgive every teacher for whatever faults they have. Protect the children and us from the evil one. Forgive us, Jesus.'

The second shameful deed I did happened when my sister Hermie (my second-eldest sister who lived in Virginia in the Free State) and her husband were visiting. Now what I did was not intentional. I was sitting on top of my mother's wardrobe fooling around or something. Then I discovered these notes. Money. I had no idea it was my sister who had hidden the money there for their journey home. I took it. I ran as fast as my feet could carry me to the record shop. I bought myself the 7-single *Living Doll* by Cliff Richard. I ran home and played it over and over and danced and sang in a world of total bliss.

When I saw my sister's distress at the missing money, I was distraught and admitted to my 'theft'. I was truly sorry. She forgave me. I love you, Hermie. (Hermie lost her beloved daughter and granddaughter in a car accident in January 2010.) I see with my eyes how Jesus carries her and I just worship at His feet. Oh the sorrow of those who do not know You, Father. Oh the sorrow of those who know You.

John 16:33 says, 'Here on earth you will have many trials and sorrows but take heart because I have overcome the world.'

Thank you, Jesus.

About teachers

My Standard 2 or 3 (Grade 4 or 5) teacher gets first prize for humiliation tactics. Whenever it was time for Maths to begin she would call me to the front, draw a circle on the board and tell me to put my nose in it as I was too stupid to do Maths. So the Maths periods passed with the kids doing Maths and me building up a hate relationship with the subject that was to last a lifetime. From that time onwards I never even tried in a Maths exam. I only put my name down and handed in a blank paper. I got 0% all the way to Standard 8 (Grade 10).

Once a teacher invited me to her house for the weekend. I thought she was unbelievably rich. In the morning I washed my only pair of socks and hung them on the line. I wrung them tightly in a creased heap so as not to show the holes. Then the teacher came to show me how to hang socks. She said if I smoothed them open I would expose more fabric to the sun and they would dry more easily. She smoothed open those pushed-together socks and you could look right through them, the holes were so big. I was so embarrassed I wanted the earth to swallow me. Later I washed dishes and broke a glass. I burst into tears and felt so utterly useless. She never invited me again. I wonder why?

The little white church around the corner did not go unnoticed. I looked at the children all dressed up on a Sunday and longed to be part of that church.

When I look back, the eternal banner I see flying over La Rochelle is my prayer I prayed in the back seat of my drunken stepfather's car:

> 'Lord, if you get me home safely I promise I will say my prayers every night for the rest of my life.'

2

Orphanage

Potchefstroom (1963-1965)

> Even if my father and mother abandon me, the Lord will
> hold me close.

– PSALM 27:10

Here is a journey I remember well. A bit like Pollyanna's train trip to her aunt but there was no rich aunt waiting for me on the other side. I received a number on arrival at the orphanage. I was No. 16 out of 31 in the dormitory. I wonder what had happened to the previous No. 16?

The departure from Johannesburg station was deeply engraved in my soul and it has replayed repeatedly throughout my life. I was in the slow-moving train going to Potchefstroom to join my sister Joan and brother Dirk in the orphanage. My mother was running along the platform next to the train and hanging on to me through the window. Her sobs were tearing both our hearts out of our bodies. My mother did love me.

From then on I pined for my mother and my brother Dale through endless lonely nights.

You can put a diamond into a milk shake and shake it all day if you like but the stone will not become part of that milk shake. Or what did the man from La Mancha sing? Whether the picture hits the stone or the stone hits the picture, it is going to be bad for the picture anyway. I was the picture.

Planet orphanage. The only recognizable thing on this planet was my sister Joan. Dear and wonderful Joanie. Joanie, who made my bed and fixed my cupboard and carried my toiletries back to their place. Joanie, who scrubbed my floor and kept me protected from the 'Gestapo'. Joanie, who saw to it that I was dressed and where I should be at the right time. In case you don't realise it; I came from a life of movies and dreams and a place where the words 'rules', 'clock' and 'time' did not exist. I had a method of astral travel known only to me. My freedom was in my head and no one knew where to find it. As for schooling and those other real things, I still refused to negotiate on it.

I was repeating Standard 6 (Grade 8). The homework time enforced upon me in the big study hall gave me wonderful space and time to write my own stories. My imagination took flight. The Pied Piper looked stupid next to me. The little children from other dormitories became my audience. I drew them into my world of make-believe. I took them into places that surprised me. I would get to a spot where I had no idea how the main character would get out of the situation as every door was closed. I would change my voice, make my eyes big, give pauses and then … the words and the solutions would flow. Sometimes they had to come back the next day to hear what happened next.

My protector, Joanie, was in her last year of school when I came to the orphanage. She wrote her Matric and was ready to go into the big wide world — leaving me behind. Only then did I realize just how much she had been carrying me.

The punishments were fast and furious. My unforgivable crimes: late for dinner; left my toothbrush in the bathroom; did not straighten the blankets on the hollow bed; my wooden floor was not shining; late for line-up …. The few cents we got for pocket money were permanently taken away from me and I was always on the receiving end of whatever punishment was handed out. I was never rebellious, mean or nasty. I had great respect for my elders; it was just that I was not made of material that fits into an institution.

One afternoon I went into the mealie fields, as I often did. Nature had this secret attraction for me. This was my stage. The mealies were my audience. I danced and acted and basked in the wind's applause. By the time I went 'home' there was an inquisition waiting for me. I had to explain where I had been and whom I had met in the mealie fields. No one understood my language so I was severely punished and humiliated as I had no interest in the obscenities I was accused of.

I met another new enemy — hunger. Suddenly I was always so hungry. I am sure the food was sufficient but somehow the growing body and starving soul could not be satisfied. The kitchen lady kindly provided dry crusts at night and our taste buds imagined they were cakes.

My nickname was 'Porcelain'. The other kids called me 'the porcelain doll' because they said I thought I was better than they were. I know I did not fit in. I did not think I was better than them but I was so different from them. One of the kind members of the staff there once told Joan and me that we had more 'class' because the first years of our lives had been happy.

But God in his kindness has provided a wonderful friend for me. It is strange how I have always had one wonderful friend. A soulmate. Even now, at the age of 60, Eliza is my wonderful friend and soulmate.

I never was a quitter. The school organized a big walk. It was really a very long walk. The girls all had to be picked up by car on the way there. I walked all the way there and all the way back. My feet were bleeding and my cheap shoes stuck to my skin but I never give up on something I start. Once I give my word I never go back on it. I was the only one from the orphanage to finish. Then I still had to walk back from the school. I do remember the lonely feeling as I entered the orphanage gates. Somehow I wished for a hero's welcome but no one was interested.

I saved a girl's life — I did! The orphanage kids had a day out at Potchefstroom dam. I saw a girl in trouble in the water. I was not a good swimmer. My swimming consisted of pretending to be a beautiful Pharaoh's daughter bathing in luxury, or some other story. But when I saw this girl's panic I jumped in from the little concrete island and swam towards her. She clung to me. I swam my 'frog stroke' as best I could, but felt her weight together with my weight and the island seemed to move further and further away. I never gave up. When we got near the island an adult took her from me. Everyone crowded around the saved girl. No one looked at me. That night when we got home it was the same thing once more: I again wished for a hero's welcome but no one was interested. I know it did not matter as I held these things in my heart. And it was good.

But some things were very bad. One of them was the day when, on my birthday, the bookkeeping teacher decided to hit me on my hands, as a birthday gift.

The custard pudding the orphanage gave us once a month, dosed with castor oil. Oh, the terrible tummy pains it gave me. I would hide in the toilets at school vowing I would never have children if it was as sore as that.

The time I was so cold, as the snow we played in melted and my clothes were wet. It was so cold that I cried. The winters were always very cold. We were allowed to warm a stone on the big stove in the kitchen and carry the warm stone in our pockets on the way to school. (Like your Word warms my heart, Jesus.)

I did not have an orphanage friend at school. My friend was a girl we called 'Uiltjie'. She always brought me sandwiches which her mom had made.

Children with moms and dads were like gods to us orphans.

The orphanage nurse was very nice to us. I once pretended to be sick just to be with her in the little hospital. Kindness was worth more than gold.

Once, my Maths teacher was so nice to me. She asked me to take some money to the office for her. I felt so wonderful to have someone's trust. I loved her even though I did no school work for anyone. By now I was so far behind that I would not know how to build without a foundation.

There were many sad moments, like my gripping on to the burglar bars in front of the little windows where I pleaded with God to forgive me for my sins and take me back to my mother. I pined for her. My mother was very good to my sister and me while we were there. She sent us a parcel every month. Receiving a parcel with biscuits and sweets was like receiving a Mercedes. The other children regarded us as being rich and very lucky. Their parents had forgotten about them.

One day my mother, brother and stepfather came to visit me at the orphanage. They were allowed to take me to the dam for the day. I was beside myself with joy. I wanted to hold on to my mother and brother and never let them go. They asked permission for me to go with them for the night.

Permission was refused. When the car drove out of the orphanage grounds I was hysterical. If I had known what God's plans were for me I would not have fallen to pieces that day. I have since learnt that nothing can happen to us which God does not sanction. All things work out for the good for those who love Him. But then I did not know it. I could not bear to go back to the room with the burglar bars and to being No. 16. I did not know it but I was scratching my face and left long bleeding scratch marks down my cheeks. The pain inside was so severe that the outside pain went unnoticed. I wonder how it is that we don't die when pain is so severe.

Death of my father, Dirk Kemp

I don't know when this happened or how I felt about it. It must have been round about this time that I got the news that my father had died. I did not know the man. Since the day I had tried to walk in his footprints I had heard from him only once.

On that occasion he told me he wanted nothing to do with me because I had chosen to stay with my mother and stepfather. Did this man not know that I had no choice in that matter? The news got worse: He had committed suicide. I decided to put that information into the bag with all the other secrets that are never to be told or thought about.

The orphanage concert

Big event! The orphanage was to present a concert! All the staff had to present an item along with the kids. I auditioned for everything and got chosen for everything. The night of the concert there was not one item without me in it. OK, except for the minister's daughter who sang an operatic song. I had nothing to do with that.

Aunty Ricky had a lot to do with the concert. She was a dear child of Jesus who had a special place in her heart for Joan and me. I think it was she who had said we had 'class'. She is still in Joan's life and I saw her at my sister Jean's funeral as well as during Joan's sickness in 2010.

'... God our Savior, who wants everyone to be saved and to understand the truth. For there is only one God and one Mediator who can reconcile God and humanity – the man Christ Jesus (1 Tim 2:3–5).

Conversion

Before the concert I have just described, there was a major happening in my life. This was the event that changed my entire life and gave it a new dimension. This is the point when I started living. This is what everything was working towards. My Father in heaven was about to introduce me to Jesus. I had no idea Jesus was real. I had no idea that a person could have a relationship with Jesus and then because of Him, with God. I knew lots of religious people. Very religious, horrible people. A minister who would judge us orphans in church. A minister who taught us about a very angry God who was going to rip us apart because our parents were bad. A minister who hit us on our hands because we did not learn our catechism verses.

These religious people did not know Jesus at all. They also did not know that Jesus was colour-blind. He loved the black people just as much as the white people. He loved the poor just as much as He loved the rich. I was so excited about Jesus. Where did I meet this Jesus? He is everywhere but He arranged a special meeting place for me. Somebody paid for me to go to a Christian camp.

I was chosen out of the whole orphanage to go to this camp. I must have been so happy to be away from the rules. How do I explain when things happen in the Spirit and you see the Creator of creation? And He sees you.

'I give them eternal life, and they will never perish. No one can snatch them away from me. For my Father has given them to me. And he is more powerful than anyone else' (John 10:28).

My prayer is that as you read this, the same Spirit will give you a heart to understand and that you will hear Jesus call your name and you will invite Him in.

The lady who led me to the Lord at this camp was 'Tannie' Grietjie Baumbach.

Life would never be the same again! Not long after this, 'Tannie' and 'Oom' Baumbach would intervene in my life in a dramatic way which I will describe shortly.

At the camp I went into a little tent and poured out my heart to God. He knew all about me and He loved me. This is like no other love. It fills the emptiness in your soul. This is the only love that fits into that hole. Nothing can separate us from God's love.

'Can anything ever separate us from Christ's love?

Does it mean he no longer loves us

if we have trouble,

or calamity,

or are persecuted,

or hungry,

or destitute,

or in danger,

or threatened with death? (As the Scriptures say, "for Your sake we are killed every day; we are being slaughtered like sheep.")

No, despite all these things,

overwhelming victory is ours through Christ, who loved us.

And I am convinced that nothing can ever separate us from God's love.

Neither death not life,

Neither angels nor demons,

Neither our fears for today

Nor our worries about tomorrow –

Not even the powers of hell can separate us from God's love.

No power in the sky above or in the earth below –

Indeed, nothing in all creation will ever be able to separate us from the love of God that is revealed in Christ Jesus our Lord'

(Rom 8:35–39).

Nor stripping, nor a suspended jail sentence, or divorce or anything you think is too big; no, none of these things can separate you from God's love.

By the time I went back to the orphanage I was ready to live for Jesus. I wanted nothing to do with the concert and I wanted everyone to know about Jesus. Aunty Ricky explained to me that we could be in show business or any business and do it to the glory of God. So there I was, in every act of the concert evening. I made such an impression that some unknown person sponsored me to have drama lessons. Once a week I went by bike to the other side of Potchefstroom for drama lessons.

Then one day soon after this an old Ford car pulled up in front of the orphanage office. A grey-haired couple in their 60s got out. It was Oom and Tannie Baumbach! My ship had arrived. My bags were packed. God had good plans for my life. This old couple fetched me and took me out of that orphanage for good and I ended up on a farm that was to become my idea of heaven. God is Good!!!!!!!!!!!

Swartruggens here I come!

The trip from the orphanage had its moments. We stopped over at the home of Tannie Baumbach's brother. He was a professor at Potchefstroom University. There was a girl my age there too, but I can't remember how she was related to them. She and I were gorging ourselves on fruit. I was so full, I wanted to pop. This girl told me that when she overate she just stuck her finger down her throat and then she could start eating from scratch again. I did this and could not believe what a relief it was. Bad thing! The start of being bulimic!

(Only years later did God cure me completely of this disease.)

3

New life

Swartruggens (1966-1968)

I arrived at Swartruggens an uncut stone and ended up blossoming into the Head Girl of Rodeon High School there. Then I went on to get a first class pass in Matric and to achieve a teacher's diploma. Only by the grace of God is that possible.

Please don't tell me about positive thinking or that Jesus is good for some people as He serves as a crutch or provides them with the positive thinking that brings out the power that lies within all of us. Where is the power of positive thinking when you lie crushed in the metal hand of a car accident? When your spirit is ready to leave your body, may you remember to call on the powerful name of Jesus. Where is the power of positive thinking when you lie in a coma in the grip of meningitis that munches away at your brain? I saw this with my own eyes in the case of my sister.

My beloved sister Joan's doctors gave instructions to the nursing staff to phone us to come to say goodbye to her. The scans showed such severe brain damage that he believed that if she lived she would be a vegetable. Now let me tell you something; it is no positive thinking that made the doctor hear Joan say, 'Good morning, Doctor Le Roux.' It was my sister coming out of her coma and even recognizing her doctor. This is God Almighty at work! This is the result of prayer! This is to glorify God! She took her first steps and even sent me an SMS. She recovered fully and she is a walking, living miracle. But the true miracle happened before she went into the coma, when she phoned me and cried out with a longing for God. She asked for forgiveness of her sins and dedicated her life to God. So you see, even if her body had died, the true miracle was her salvation and God was glorified! There is much more to this, but that is Joanie's testimony.

Another lesson I had to learn was that having Jesus in your life did not mean the end of trials. They come in continuously just as the waves on the shore; one after the other. It is so important to stay in the Word or the devil will pull you away before you even know it.

My foster parents — the Baumbachs

Swartruggens is surrounded by churches — the kind made from bricks and stone. These churches are easy to tell by their shape. Jesus talks about another church, the one kept inside a body of flesh and blood. These are also easy to tell by their fruit but in truth only Jesus knows whose names are written in the Book of Life.

Oom Baumbach

Oom Baumbach was one of the easy ones to tell. His fruits were so pure anyone could tell. I knew for sure the one morning when he woke me up as usual. That morning he first covered my body which had slipped out of my pyjama top, before waking me. This was the first 'Jesus' person I met. Oom Baumbach would walk me to the farm bus every morning. Whatever my hormonal mood, it never changed his loving attitude. He always told me stories which he had read in the Bible or in the *Huisgenoot* magazine. He also knew everything about anything but he was the type of man who would tell you in such a way that you would think that it was you that had informed him.

It was he who helped me with my homework — ever patient and ever lifting me up. He brought me to a point where I could not wait to go to school because all my work was done. He showed me how interesting schoolwork was: That it was all the wonderful knowledge God had put there for us to uncover. We do not go to school or work to get, but to give and by giving we receive. I am so glad I met Jesus in the form of a man. It was he who okayed it when I came with a stupid request. He let me learn by myself and never criticized. I was putting on weight as I was eating everything put in front of me. When my image in the mirror shocked me I requested no more big meals at breakfast and said that I needed more help. I wanted a plastic body suit I saw in a magazine to help me in the weight-shedding process. Tannie Baumbach told me just how stupid I was, but Oom Baumbach spoke to her and allowed the silly request. Oom Baumbach never fell over my suitcase in the middle of my room and never minded it being there. Tannie Baumbach would bump into it daily and never stopped nagging me. (Or so it seemed at that time.)

Tannie Baumbach

Tannie Baumbach had her name carved in the Book of Life but her old nature was not going to lie down and be silenced. But our Heavenly Father knows how to use the cheek of the old self to achieve in the new self. She was a domineering leader who stopped at nothing. She insisted on being in the front but it is there in the front that she got things done. What sort of woman fosters a 15-year-old, at the age of 60? One with hair on her teeth or with the Spirit in her heart. She founded an old age home in Swartruggens. I think it is called the Grietjie Baumbach Old Age Home.

It was she who planted the evangelical seed in my heart although it was she who almost killed the same seed. She ran a little farm shop from the house. This was to help the black workers who had no transport, to buy the essentials. But the one thing this shop did not have was kindness. I uttered one of those well-known sentences 'How can she be a Christian and talk like that to people because they are black?' I have since learnt that all of us have a 'How can you be a Christian if … ?' side to us. God in his mercy is busy with each one of us and if we are looking for a Christian who does not disappoint us, to bring us to heaven, then we will surely burn in hell. That is why God sent Jesus to us. Jesus said 'Follow me!' What is it to you what happens to others?

Later, in my dancing years I still had contact with Tannie Baumbach until one day when she saw me, she was so insulting about my ageing appearance that I decided I did not want to ever see her again. Her tongue was like a dagger. The last time this dagger got to me, I was in a backslidden life, far away from Jesus. With Him I would have understood who she was, have hurt for a while and then just handed the matter over to Him. I bet if she were still alive, she could have added a character sketch of me here that would make me blush. I will tell a bit of it on her behalf. I could really withdraw. I could really be difficult and full of anger. I remember when a male Christian friend of the Baumbachs visited for a weekend and saw my long face and ungrateful behaviour, that the only compliment he could pay me as he left was to thank me for my physical beauty. I felt very ashamed.

I also did not want my foster father to kiss me 'Good morning' or 'Hello'. I could not bear the physical closeness of a man near me. When I get to heaven I am going to embrace my foster father and hold him and give him a big smacker of a kiss full on his mouth. I have asked Jesus many times since returning to Him, to please embrace my foster parents and to thank them. I know that they know that the work they had done for Jesus, with me, was not in vain. The imprint they left on me turned out to be the strongest of my entire lifetime. The God print. Thank you Oom and Tannie Baumbach. Your input has eternal value and will not burn in the fire.

Schooldays in Swartruggens

I had come a long way, by the grace of God, from that first day at high school in Swartruggens.

My head hung low. I was two years older than my classmates. I had to repeat Standard 8 (Grade 10). I looked at the children around me. I had so many shameful secrets. They were so normal. I wished to be like them but was still covered in 'goo' from a traumatic past. My foster mother and father prayed. This couple's prayers carried me through a long life of backsliding. God was teaching me to hear his Voice in his Word and to obey it.

'For God so loved the world that He gave His only begotten Son, that whoever believes in Him should not perish but have everlasting life' (John 3:16, NKJV).

Suddenly I saw my classmates as being very precious to God. As precious as I was! Jesus showed me how to treat others as I would like them to treat me. He showed me that I must stop wanting a friend, but to be a friend. What a valuable lesson this was. I started to look away from myself and looked at others with eyes that see and ears that hear. I made notes of their birthdays and read up on topics that interested them. I started to pray for those near me. My whole world turned around. I was suddenly laughing with others. I was part of groups. I started to love those around me.

Glenda Kemp in Grade 12 at Rodeon High School

The biggest connection with me and Swartruggens was the farm; the hills, the trees, the river, the dam, the cows and the donkey cart. There was no telling where it ended and I began. This was a 'Dagwood' of open space and freedom.

Everything became a personality — me and the 'mountain'. I would start the climb to the top and did not allow myself to look back until I reached the very top. Then I would close my eyes, turn around and tell myself: If you open your eyes now, you will see God's gift to you. You must take in the smells, the wind on your skin, the sight and the feeling. Hold it as you would hold on to God's Word. Store it in your heart. How this enhanced my experience. I do that at the beach today. I do that to the Word. I have become a 'word-tasting connoisseur'. I get drunk with the gift of the Spirit. The joy of the Lord is my strength.

Then there was me and the special tree that branched over the little stream. Telling about these experiences is like going back onto holy ground. Having Nature opened to you and standing in awe, and knowing that you could never describe this to anyone. You have to be alone with God to hear what you see; to see what you hear. I can relate to Paul in the Bible when he says he does not know if he was in the Spirit or in the body, except that I know that I was in the body but that I could see with the Spirit. You don't have to be in Nature to live this. You have to be in God's Word and as you get to know Him and start to walk with Jesus, you start to read in the Spirit. I don't know how to relive this without wanting to push Jesus forward so you can look at Him. It is He who opens eyes and hearts. I don't know how to say anything without talking about Him. I love Him so much, because He loved me first; while I was yet a sinner. All this beauty from the farm makes me so grateful that I want to cry happy tears all over the page. And even today, I live by the sea and read the sun, the sea and sand every day. God's mercies are new every morning.

Let's get back to things. Things like first love. I fell in love with Felix the first time our eyes locked in the school corridor. This was to be the make or break of my day. Then one day he stopped and said, 'Hallo, pretty thing.' He looked into my eyes and it burnt right through to my toes. I was never the same again. I lived for those encounters. We became an 'item'. He was in Matric and I was in Standard 8 (Grade 10). He played rugby for the school's first team and he used my heart as a ball. And later I found out he did that with a few other girls' hearts as well.

But while it lasted it was wonderful. The first time he kissed me after a movie I wrote it in my diary and relived it a million times. He was the man I wanted to marry but only by God's rules. Our first fight was when he visited me on the farm and did not look away when I climbed over a fence. My foster father, ever the gentleman, always looked away, as a girl's dress would lift up and show more leg than was respectable. Felix did not look away. My body was a temple of God and only to be given away to the man who would be my husband, and only to be seen by the man who was to be my husband.

Don't forget, the stepfather episode had been wiped away by Jesus. He had made me holy and pure as only the Son of God can.

Felix went away to the army in Heidelberg. I received a few very strange 'love letters'. He always addressed me as 'dog'. My poor foster parents must have prayed many nights away asking for God to intervene. I even visited the man in the army once. Then I received the last 'love letter' saying his Heidelberg girlfriend was pregnant and that he was going to marry her. Just like that. I then learnt about some of his other Swartruggens girlfriends as well. But I won't go into that. Can you believe that the weekend before this man's wedding he came to visit me and declared his love for me? By that time I was seeing what was really in front of me and I was glad to see him go.

Swartruggens is the breath of fresh air in my life. It is the story of a young girl winning debates, teaching Sunday School, participating in school plays, winning talent competitions, buying puppets and using them to raise money for the school and to explain the Bible in Sunday School, winning the hearts of her teachers and her friends and being chosen as prefect and then Head Girl of Rodeon High School. The headmaster's last words to me were: 'You will achieve much, we will hear from you again. Your name will be remembered.'

It is the story of the one starfish that was thrown back into the sea. Because of those three years of my life I knew where to go back to when my life spiralled out of control many years later. No matter that I backslid for so long, and went so far away from what my foster parents and their son Erdi Baumbach stood for. Jesus says that He will finish the good work He started, and He did. The foundation that was built here was Jesus — the true and only cornerstone.

Glenda Kemp - Snake Dancer

4

Teachers' College

1969-1971

Something went drastically wrong. If this had been an operation it would have been fatal. On my arrival at the Potchefstroom Teachers' College I was like someone carrying all these wonderful glass milk bottles as a trophy. Then suddenly I crashed into a brick wall. There is spilt milk and broken glass everywhere. I am cut. I am trying to describe my feelings about Teachers' College.

The brick wall I walked into was the initiation ceremony that lasted for three weeks but which seemed like eternity.

I was alone in a room in a hostel called Nellie Swart. No one saw the sign on my newly-planted soul that said 'keep off'. They marched on this soil with 20 elephants and 10 bulldozers. They ripped open 5 West Lane, La Rochelle and No. 16 in the orphanage. They thought they just robbed me of my sleep, but they robbed me of much more. They made us stand in a row, bent forward, running our hands through our hair all night long. They degraded us and made us say how utterly rotten we were.

How I wish the part of me that had walked until the skin stuck to my shoes, had been there. I caved in and managed to put a door, a lock and burglar bars onto that cave. I could not get out and no one could get in. Just like that little girl with the terrible secret.

During the initiation period there was never a moment to read my Father's Word and I never wanted another moment for his Word. I turned away from the only place that could have given me back who I should be. I embraced food and put on so much weight in no time that I needed a whole new wardrobe.

There was a light. Mariaan Steyn became my friend. But she was not a soulmate. We had some fun with Camelot and going to *sokkies*. It did not last long after she met a guy and I was on my own. I was asked out on dates but in the cave I found myself in, there was no key for a man to come in. I said 'No' so many times that soon no one asked me anymore. Everyone around me had partners and they were planning weddings. My heart was cold and unable to respond to any man.

I turned 21. My sister Hermie sent me my very first bouquet of flowers. That was very, very special to me.

The subject I specialized in was drama. The only time that I was alive was when we had drama. That shy girl died a sudden death. I could be anything the drama teacher wanted. There was no character or movement I could not master. The worst thing that ever happened was when the students decided to boycott (mass bunk) our drama lessons. I would silently die. The strange thing was that I was not like any of the other drama students. They were very eccentric and very loud. I was the quiet mouse until I got onto the stage. That was when I reigned.

News of a death

I was taken aside to be given the bad news that my father had died. I thought of my foster father. My reply was, 'Which father?'

On hearing it was my stepfather I was very relieved and even happy that it was not my foster father. I did not shed a tear. They asked if I wanted to go home and my answer was 'No'. My mother and my little brother, Dale, moved in with my sister Joan. They were now living in Durban.

An evening at a discotheque

My sister Jean used to drive all the way from Johannesburg to fetch me to visit her during the holidays. It was during one of these holidays or weekends that something happened that was to change my life forever: It was something that would make the whole of South Africa sit up and take notice: that would make my name a household name. I could never have imagined that an evening at the Marakesh discotheque in Hillbrow would be the beginning of something very big.

Nature and music have the same effect on me. They move me.

Someone must have asked me to dance. I was dancing. Then suddenly everyone else had stopped dancing and was watching me. They formed a circle around me, clapping as I moved. I never drank alcohol. Never throughout my entire life. I also never took drugs and I never slept around. Because I was such a loner there was no one to influence me from outside. It was the music that did it. It took different parts of my body to different places as the music demanded. To say I loved dancing and acting was an understatement.

The manager of the Marakesh offered me a job as a go-go dancer. There was a box on each side of the disc jockey's turntable. The go-go girls would stand on the box and dance for 15 minutes and then go off. That box restricted me. As no one was dancing when I was on it; it suited me to use the main dance floor to entertain the people. One night some of my tummy showed and I got such a 'Wow' reaction as the moving tummy muscles were displayed that I decided to roll up my top and roll down the waist of my pants.

When the music changed to slow dancing the other go-go girls would get off the boxes. I stayed. I let the slow music flirt with me. I moved my hands to the music as if I was taking off my clothes, bit by bit. Miming. I was drawing crowds.

My transport problem back to my sister's place was kindly solved by the manager who, at the same time, not so kindly presented me with another problem. One night he tried to kiss me and I said 'No'. Then this poor big baby of a man played a role that he thought would move me. He asked, 'Was there something wrong with me, that you did not fall for my advances?'

I explained that it had nothing to do with him. I was still a virgin and only intended sleeping with my husband. Now, had I dropped an atom bomb on Hillbrow I would have had less reaction. I became the laughing stock of the discotheque. This did not faze me. I was there to dance, and I danced every Friday and Saturday night.

There were practical obstacles to overcome. I was studying in Potchefstroom and this weekend job was in Johannesburg. So I asked for a transfer to Goudstad Teachers' College.

To Goudstad Teachers' Training College

This college in Johannesburg was where the future educators of the Afrikaners of South Africa received their training. Outward appearance was of the utmost importance. Although most students ranged in age between 20 and 25, the rules were more like those of a convent.

No trousers or slack suits were allowed for the ladies. Dresses had to be no shorter than a certain length. Seven o'clock in the evening was the time by which students had to be in the hostel and those who were even one minute late were punished.

Maybe this is what made it so unacceptable and scandalous to do what I did. I was meant to be part of this brigade. I was still doing the weekend dancing work in Hillbrow but now I had also managed to get a cocktail hour of dancing work at the President Hotel's discotheque called 'TJ 1'.

Cocktail hour was from 5:00 p.m. to 7:00 p.m. My last dance performance was at 6:45 p.m. and 7:00 p.m. was Cinderella time at the hostel.

My regular lift was not around so in desperation I grabbed the first man I saw nearest to the exit and asked him for a lift to Goudstad College. This man was Karl Koczwara — a German draughtsman. Many years later he would become my husband and the father of my wonderful daughter.

My relationship with my foster parents was slipping away. Now that I had locked Jesus up in the cupboard and was doing my own thing, I was like Adam and Eve, hiding from God.

Dancing provided me with an escape I did not know possible. Nothing else mattered when I was dancing. I lived for the music and the words and wanted to share this with whoever was looking at me. Yes, I needed the pocket money but the main reason I took more dancing work was because of the satisfaction it was giving me in escaping from my circumstances.

Here I was, a 23-year-old Afrikaner girl running around the streets of Johannesburg working as a go-go dancer.

The night club

How I ended up in this night club I don't know. I was dancing in a cage wearing a white bikini while ladies of the night handed out tickets to male customers for a dance on the dance floor.

I did not realize it was a brothel when I accepted the job. The owner was unnaturally protective of me. He allowed no one near me as I was only to do the regular dance in the cage and that was it. I remember sitting there in his office doing my Bible Academy projects for Teachers' College. This is a pattern that was to follow the whole of my ten-year dancing and stripping career. Anyone who looks back over my life will see that God placed someone there to protect me in every situation. I know that it was the prayers of my foster parents that moved the hand of God.

My new found freedom made me careless about my studies and I missed two year-end exams. One was the dreaded Maths which I could not do anyway, and they were not as lenient as at Potchefstroom. The other was a subject I knew well but I did not make it to the exam room. I passed all the other subjects and it was a formality for me to only rewrite the two subjects.

I would still be given a teaching post, but I would not receive my diploma until I rewrote those two subjects.

The teaching world was waiting. All I had to do was to wait to see where I had been placed. My studies were financed by a loan from the Education Department and in return I would have to teach wherever they placed me.

5

Dancing — the first three years

The first year of dancing (1972)

My first home and my first snakes!

Rule number one — NO DEBT! I looked at my sister Joan; she was still paying off on clothes that she no longer had. Look at my new flat! My first home that is all mine. A tiny bachelor flat. A mattress on the floor. Wooden boxes serving as table and chairs. All paid for. My humble beginnings. I had an address in the heart of Johannesburg.

Dancing work was just popping up everywhere.

In the meantime my mom and brother had moved back to Johannesburg. My mother was staying on a plot in Benoni. My brother Dale spent every weekend with me.

Dale had a new hobby. Snakes! His new found pets also found their way to my flat as guests; wanted or not. They did not impress me either way. But they did impress my landlord when my brother and his friends thought it would be funny to put the little snakes on his doorstep. If they impressed the landlord then maybe they would impress my audience.

Come Friday night, my packing included two tiny snakes together with nipple caps and g-strings. The basket I used for them to make their first appearance was my pink sewing basket all the way from Swartruggens. I appeared in a very dramatic way with the little basket balanced on my head and my hips swinging to the sound of drums. By the time I pulled out these little 'worms' the audience was on the edge of their seats. I had found a gimmick. Bring on the snakes. Bigger and better. That was my next mission.

The arrival of a telegram!

I was to teach in 'Koornfontein'. No such place on the map. Look again. Still no such place on the map. So I silently ignored the whole issue and continued dancing.

By the time the second telegram arrived I was fully employed at a restaurant called the Westerwald. The telegram said to ignore 'Koornfontein' as it was meant to be 'Doornfontein'. I should start teaching at Doornfontein in Johannesburg.

The Westerwald restaurant was a real challenge. I would dance for one year and then teach. So silently I ignored the second telegram as well.

Going onto a stage and dancing was not what I was about. Those days were over. Every performance had to have a story. A beginning, middle and an end.

I cannot remember when I did my first strip. I only remember appearing on the stage with tiny pieces of material stuck on as nipple caps and a g-string. From there I would move through a story that allowed me to act, slow dance, dance vigorously and clown my way back to being fully dressed. I was obeying the law. The law stated that you were not allowed to leave the stage wearing less clothes than you came on-stage with.

The Westerwald restaurant was about four blocks away from where I lived. It was under new ownership. On my first evening there I danced to an audience of two people. The next week the same two people were back with six friends. And so it continued. In a year's time people were turned away. Without a booking there was no way you could see this unknown woman who performed and danced her way into her clothes. The owner of the restaurant always called me 'Koos'. (Someone had suggested I have a stage name: 'Natasha'. This did not stick for me or the owner. Koos was closer to my barefoot nature than exotic Natasha.) The owner was so protective and kind to me. It was almost as if he had instructions from my foster parents and was not going to allow anyone to bother me.

My only form of transport, or let me call it four wheels, was a baby's pram: the old fashioned type with a hood. You might wonder what this is about.

I had made a new connection. Peter Curner, the professional snake collector, supplied me with a snake that was too heavy to carry but just the right size to curl up in a baby's pram. It was the most practical way for someone without a driver's licence to transport 'livestock' four blocks. I became a regular sight running down Bree Street wearing my long evening dress, pushing the pram in front of me.

I did cause the odd stir. Going down in the lift was always my stressful time, due to the silence of the lift and an audible 'shhhh' sound like a deflating tyre coming from the pram. The enclosed space left no room for any lift occupants with snake phobia.

On one occasion a lady came over to reprimand me for being out at that time of the night with my baby. I told her it was not a baby but a snake. She still continued to move towards the contents of the pram as if I had not spoken. The last I saw of her was a small figure disappearing into the night with her arms in the air while her scream still lingered.

An interesting year. My act was not the same from one week to the next. This is when I learnt what worked and what did not work. I also tried fire dancing — the hard way. I tried these different mixtures as no one would tell me the secret. I ended up burning my face in the process. I remember thinking that I was scarred for life. But it healed and I did get to doing fire dancing with the right ingredients. My own mother was now very much part of my life. I remember one night I could not put the one fire stick out in my mouth and wanted her to take it to the back to put it out. She took the stick and started dancing with it. I was very annoyed with her. My mother was an unusual woman.

One of my acts involved two dress mannequins. I had the owner and his waiters carry one big doll on to the dimly-lit stage. Then they would carry me on, as stiff as a doll, and wearing a wig. Then the next doll. All of us in g-strings and nipple caps. I would then slowly and stiffly awake. Then I would take a can of oil and oil my limbs. So I would start dancing using different parts of my body as they were oiled. The oil remained part of my show for a long time.

Another act was that of a woman washing her clothes. I then put the wet vest on and danced wearing it as part of the show.

African dancing was what moved me most. The drums could beat with my heart.

Then of course the puppets from Swartruggens — the little devil puppet trying to pull my clothes off.

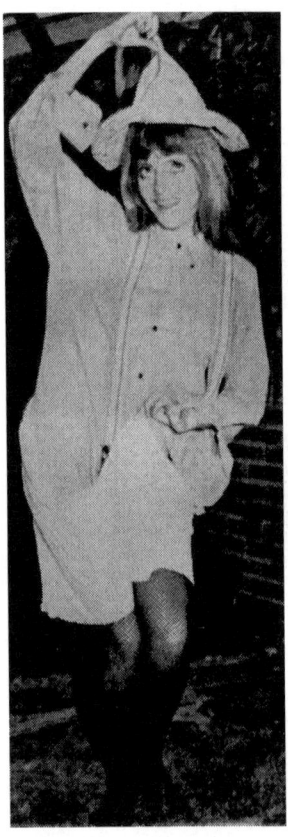

Humorous start to the show

(I find it hard describing these actions knowing that Jesus is sitting here next to me.)

I had a formula: Always start and end the show with humour. I had very big bloomers I wore with braces and a real *Voortrekker kappie* which a friend of Tannie Baumbach had made for me to wear for protection against the sun while I explored the countryside round the farm.

While at the Westerwald restaurant I was asked to dance at the Rand Easter Show and other functions. An entertainment magazine seemed to pick up on me. I appeared in its pages on a regular basis. I was also finding my face (or my body) in the newspapers. Before long I was the centre spread in an Afrikaans magazine called *Keur* and then *Scope* followed. There was lots of modelling work. I loved what I was doing and I know I was very good at it. I put my heart into every performance. I always said I would stop the day I stopped enjoying it.

I moved to a bigger flat just around the corner from the previous one. My sister Joan moved from Durban to stay with me. She was going through the pains of a bad relationship. It was wonderful to have my sister living with me. She was my secretary and helped to organize things, almost like when we were in the orphanage. The two of us watched movies every day and all day long. She was my best friend. She still is.

The second year of dancing (1973)

One-bedroomed flat in Paulshof — second home

Enter at own risk. I should have had an indemnity form signed before entering. One unsuspecting visitor ended up on the table screeching like a

My first big snake

lady when encountering a mouse. Why the commotion? Well there was the snake; which was to be expected. The first question asked was always, 'Is the snake locked up?' 'Yes'.

'Oupa', the snake, lived in a display cabinet covered with glass with holes in the shelves which allowed him to move around but he was not given the freedom of the flat. No one asked if 'Likkie', the *leguaan*, was locked up. Likkie had the freedom of the town. Likkie found his favourite spot under a bit of surplus carpet that crept up the wall. He did not take kindly to visitors who screamed when he was out on an exercise run around the flat. It confused him and made him run towards the visitor when in fact he wanted to get away.

The Likkie I fell in love with was only a tiny little lizard when I brought him home. He was one of the 'finds' that Peter Curner collected. This man was now providing me with a 'swap-your-snake' service. When the strain became too much for a slithering python we would exchange him like a library book. Each time I got a new snake he would also be named 'Oupa', like his predecessor.

Keeping Likkie was now like having a medium-sized crocodile running around the flat. Things were getting a bit unhygienic. Likkie would have to go. When I arrived with my pet at the Johannesburg Zoo I could hardly speak as my sobs interrupted my story. The zoo keepers were having their lunch. Many times when I explained my situation it sounded too strange to be true. Then when I opened the container, a bewildered Likkie sprayed his digested breakfast contents all over the zoo workers and their lunch.

I did return later to visit my leguaan. As I leaned over the wall round the enclosure, I called his name and expected to see Likkie running to me with his little tongue flicking in and out. What I saw was hundreds of leguaans with their tongues flicking in and out. If only I had put a ribbon on his neck I might have had some hope of recognizing him. So that was the end of the leguaans. Luckily for him it was a good ending.

There were more animals. It was the snakes' fault. The pet shop sold me rabbits to feed to the snakes. As if that was going to happen! I cuddled up with the rabbit and wondered why snakes don't eat bacon and eggs and pap like we do. So the next thing on the snakes' menu was little chicks. They also turned out to be far too soft and cuddly so they were added to the list of snake food pets. Big chickens did not give me an affectionate look and I called them 'Kentucky'. But I was not going to be an eyewitness to them doing their bit in the food chain. So I would throw the chicken on the shelf furthest away from the snake, lock the cage and Joan and I would run to the movies. We would make sure we visited two tearoom cinemas where you could watch two double feature movies and have two cool drinks thrown in for the price of one. By that time it was safe to return to the flat. The only sign of Kentucky would be a very big hump in the snake's body.

The third year of dancing (1974)

The biscuit tin — operation savings

Conventionality was not part of my set-up. Goal: Buy a house. The flat was getting too small. The snake food was running all over the place and my mom, Dale (my younger brother), my older brother Dirk and my sister Jean were often there with Joan and me.

This is the story of a house that came out of a biscuit tin. When we found the house we wanted in Parkmore, Sandton, I emptied the biscuit tin's

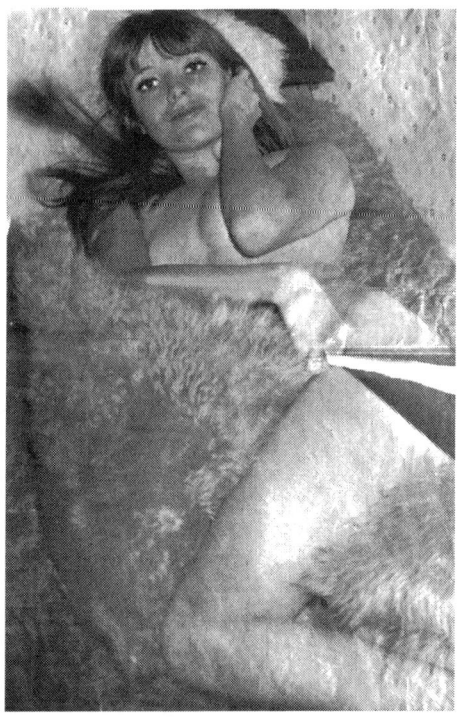

My first pin-up

contents onto the estate agent's desk. The full amount in cash. Bank notes collected from modelling, calendar pin-ups, centre spreads, cabaret, strip shows, promotions at shopping centres, opening of conventions, dancing on water beds in shopping centres, advertising toilets, and cabaret in Rhodesia (now Zimbabwe). Every cent was put into a biscuit tin and the notes were bound together in thousands with elastic bands. Of course the estate agents thought this was newsworthy and called up the press. There was my biscuit tin, my home, my house and my face on the front page — again. The attention this

attracted was not what I was hoping for. I got a call from the Receiver of Revenue. So I did what was the right thing to do and paid my taxes.

My first house — a psychiatrist's dream thesis! A house overflowing with siblings in search of lost relationships.

Three sisters and a brother and their children. Plasters for broken hearts and lost dreams. The house was so full that the only place my bed could fit in was in the garage! So that is where I slept; in the garage!

Let's pause in the story of my third year of dancing for a travel interlude.

6

America

Amerca? Did someone say America? My head was spinning. America was very big and in my mind, placing it next to Swartruggens, it was enormous. I felt like a little girl who was going to get dressed in her mother's clothes. Negotiations were taking place. Destination: Boston. I was going to be a star. And without the snake.

There was a lot to prepare. Here I was, the little 'orphan' from Swartruggens, on my first overseas flight. Everything was new. Not always a nice new. I wondered why they showed silent movies on the airplane. I only discovered on later flights that I was meant to purchase headphones.

I asked the air hostess on the Alitalia flight if I could have some milk for my tea. She stared at me as if I had escaped from a lunatic asylum. She picked up a little packet and asked me what I thought that was? It was powdered milk.

The stopover in Rome almost brought my dreams crashing down. I had no visa. A young Italian official came to the rescue of this damsel in distress. I have no idea how he solved the problem but I was the last passenger to embark for the flight to America. My hero ran with me and presented me with a rose as I reached the area where he had to stay behind. Sometimes it was profitable to be young and pretty.

Don't ask me why, but I thought anything outside of South Africa would be like a funfair. Bricks were bricks and tar was black. People were marching with banners: We didn't want blacks in our buses. Huh? This was Boston?

The dark stairs going down to a basement flat turned out to be the home of a lovely single mom and her four-year-old daughter. Elegance and hospitality made up for the lack of daylight. I was welcomed and felt safe and secure in what was to be my home in Boston. Another answer to my foster parents' prayers?

It was with much anticipation that I packed my show bag. How would I compare to the other ladies? What was waiting for me?

What was waiting for me!!! I could rename my life: You won't believe what happened to me! I don't know how long it took me to realize I was employed in a brothel. The ladies of the night surrounded the alien from the other planet; that alien was me. They asked me, 'Why are you white?', 'Where did you get shoes from?' and 'How do you get through the lions when you go to the airport?'

I knew that I was in big trouble. As it is with these places it was rather dark. I had an unbelievable desire to run and never stop. Instead of running, my legs stayed put as my eyes looked at the first 'show' on a little stage. Dancing was of no interest. The girl undressed and showed what was up for sale. I was taken to the dressing room upstairs and told to mix with men in between shows. I was not allowed to stay in the dressing room. And I thought I had talent. The continuous sound of dragging jazz music seemed sticky. It stuck on everything and made it dark. It was light to my heart when the beat of my South African *Ipi Tombi* music started. I went on to that little stage and acted and danced my heart out. The whole place came to a halt. Wrong place, wrong show. You don't eat caviar in McDonald's. The *Click Song* was next. I picked up a glass of oily 'champagne' and had it slide from my mouth down my body. Oil sinking into my skin and my hair.

My hair. I had to wash my hair. I washed my hair. Men had bought tickets to see me. I washed my hair. I was wanted downstairs. I washed my hair. By the time I managed to get the oil out of my hair it was time for my next show. And the next oil. And I had to wash my hair.

This story could have been a tragedy. But I had my foster parents praying for me! Oh the power of prayer. The protective angel stepped in. The owner took me under his wing. He saw the child in the 25-year-old body and gave strict orders that I was out of bounds. He allowed me to end my contract after one month and sent me off to wash my hair.

I could not come home without having experienced New York. So there I was on my way to the Big Apple for a weekend. One look at the never-ending rise and fall of the people-covered streets made me seasick. 'Don't quit,' I told myself. Before running for cover I had to see the Empire State Building and Central Park. The 'Empire State Building' engraved ashtray would serve as proof that I was there. That is until you turn it around and see 'Made in China'. Now Central Park, and then a place to stay for the night. Could it be that this place called New York had people everywhere that had the same face? I could swear I had seen this man at the airport, and then at the Empire State Building and now at Central Park? OK, so I was being followed. My education at that stage did not include losing a stalker. The most practical thing that came to mind was to stop a taxi, go back to the airport and back to my host in Boston. Guess what? I had been to New York!

And then I was home.

Never mind New York — although that was a physical experience, I want to tell you about spiritual experience.

Spiritual experience is when you stand before the Word and God says to you — 'Do it!'

'… if someone asks for your coat, give your undercoat too. … Walk the extra mile (Matt 5:40–41).

You are going through a divorce and you obey God. You don't ask for his pension money and you agree to pay out for a house from money you don't have. That is experience. When you see how God provides and even more when He does not provide and you experience his presence in the pain.

Experience is when your employer tells you to do something which is the last straw that breaks the camel's back. You run to God and God says: 'You work for Me, not for her.' God gets your attention and the 'broken back' is what brings you to the next place. To change your season.

Experience is when someone smashes your car's headlight that needed replacing anyway. You think God in his kindness is letting her pay for your light. Then God tightens the guilt around your throat until you pick up the phone and in utter humiliation confess that the light was broken in the first place and return the lady's money.

> 'Fools make fun of guilt, but the godly acknowledge it and seek reconciliation' (Prov 14:9).

That is experience.

Read and obey.

Your ultimate reward is getting ever closer to Jesus. To be able to say 'My sheep know my voice,' is the truth!

7

Back home

Things that fly high

I was spreading my wings. Looking at a recent newspaper clipping brought back memories of things that flew high to get me to where the demand was.

'Hissteria' on flight 514 (1972)

The SAA flight 514 from Durban to Johannesburg was doing what a flight does when it is ready for take-off. The snake was doing what a snake does when encountering flight vibrations.

I was doing what it would be expected I should be doing; trying to keep the lid on the basket by my feet. The right thing to do would have been to sit on the basket but this was not possible as I was strapped down in the seat ready for take-off. The position of my body took the strength off my foot on the basket and the python who was on his own mission, found the foot pressure weak

One beady eye looked my fellow passenger in the face.

Pandemonium.

I told them not to worry — it is only a snake! Does no one ever listen? Or maybe that was the problem; they did listen.

By now a long neck attached to the beady eyes was lifting the lid and the revelation was more than my fellow passengers could handle.

Sssssssssssuch a sssssssssshame.

The rest I will leave to your imagination.

The plane's engines powered down. The doors reopened. I was escorted out of the plane. The snake was relocated to the hold. I was allowed to re-enter the plane. The plane was delayed.

This story was the first to ever hit the tabloids telling of an unknown young woman, Glenda Kemp, who kept company with a python in a basket on her travels around South Africa.

High hitch-hike

Some people are reliable and some people are 'stupidly reliable'. I am 'stupidly reliable'.

When the booking agent made a mistake and booked me on a flight taking off from Lanseria Airport when it should have been from Jan Smuts Airport, I did not allow that to keep me grounded. An appointment is an appointment and a promise is a promise. This has nothing to do with money, it is about integrity. A show is booked and a show will take place. The flight I should have been on had already left Jan Smuts Airport and I was at Lanseria.

Desperate action: 'Any pilots around flying to Swaziland?'

Someone was willing to give me a lift to Swaziland in his plane. I have no recollection of the pilot because the one thing that stood out about this flight was that the pilot had to climb out of this little plane to go to the front and manually pull down on the little propeller to get it to start. Was I going to die in the line of duty? Would there be a body to bury? Once we were up in the sky the propeller managed to remain turning so it was a case of *All's Well That Ends Well.* The show must go on.

One woman's husband is another woman's pilot

A weekend trip to an island in Mozambique. Deep sea fishing. All expenses included. No strings attached. Blissful holiday without having to remove any clothing. This was a wonderful invitation and I accepted it.

I joined a few men for the take-off. This private plane was more stable than the one I had flown to Swaziland in.

The island was perfect; my room was perfect and the company was perfect. All promises were kept and my room was my own and the company was nothing but company. The gentleman and the lady.

My first deep sea fishing trip and I was not seasick.

All good things come to an end. What an end this trip came to. My host, the pilot, signed the necessary documents on our return to Lanseria airport. I stood next to him as he did so. Then from nowhere a woman appeared and started hitting him over the head with something. She screamed abuse at the top of her voice. After finishing with him she turned to me. 'This is my husband ....' We won't repeat the names she called me. I tried to assure her that I was only a guest and had no personal relationship with her husband.

Doing the work I do, and having the reputation I had, I would have had more luck explaining I was actually Father Christmas.

I witnessed an innocent man being found guilty and I had no way of helping him.

I hope the truth did prevail somewhere along the line and that this wife's torment was lifted.

Glenda v Glenda

Going away from home was not my idea of fun. But instead of saying 'No,' I just said, 'I want R500 a night.' A 'Yes' to this meant packing and travelling, much to my annoyance.

For a woman who did not drink, did not smoke and certainly did not sleep around, going away meant keeping company with loneliness. My profession put me in the centre of a world that had no attractions for me. Drinking people, late nights and noise did not get my vote; performing and dancing sure did. When the last note of my music disappeared, so did I.

It was on the beach at Port Elizabeth, where I was using the sun and sea to pass the time before my next performance, that the strangest invitation came my way. This is the clearest story to paint a picture of how the stripper Glenda and the private Glenda differed.

There was this young man who managed to worm his way into my presence. He must have done something right because I normally had a way of making it clear that I wanted to be alone. He picked up the courage to ask me out on a date. Would I accompany him tonight to the Glenda Kemp show? I must have changed colour and lost my voice. He read this as embarrassment. Which it was, but not in the way he thought. He then went on to apologize profusely as he realized that I was not the type of girl to go to that type of performance. He was sorry to have insulted me. We parted company with only one of us knowing the truth. I often wondered if there was any realization on his part or recognition of me when he watched Glenda Kemp perform that night.

This was not an unusual experience. I would have people come to the house to bring a deposit and ask to see Glenda Kemp. When I said that I was Glenda Kemp, they would insist that they wanted to see the stripper. I did not look as if I could cause a storm in a teacup, never mind a country. I can explain this last comment.

About my shows

I played the part of a stripper. And I played it very well. This stripper could go to places I would never have dared to go to. This stripper could have imaginary partners and flow into a sensual world of embraces while a whole audience was peeping through a keyhole. That was part of the show. The rest was fun and athleticism. I remember Anneline Kriel (Miss South Africa 1974), remarking after attending a private show that my body was not sexy but athletic. My shows had nudity and sensuality but never pornography. When I was in the nude I made use of an oil lamp. It threw out circles of different coloured lights which blended into one another. I would be in the centre of the light and my body would appear to be coloured with moving oil colours. I would try to flow as if I were one of the bubbles. The other light was the strobe. I would set it at a speed that made me move in stages. I would move very fast but the audience had the impression that I was moving in slow motion. But while they were still looking at one spot my image was already in another spot and another position. Then when the light returned to a normal soft red light I would stand there like a young girl totally embarrassed at being in front of an audience. I would get dressed shyly in my big bloomers and *Voortrekker kappie* or a schoolgirl outfit, and wave and smile goodbye.

Photos were not allowed as that would freeze the naked moment out of its context.

My biggest mistake was when I starred in a movie depicting my life. I allowed filming without my usual lighting. This put the whole performance in a bright light, devoid of the lighting I used as clothing in my shows. I have never watched the movie as it is shown today and never will. This is a case of the past catching up with you. I did watch the South African version without the nudity. It was supposedly my life story but at that time I was not ready to expose my life to the world and we just made up most of the story. This book is from my own hand and as it was for me. The reason I am putting my life into print is because I have again been approached to do a movie on my life and this time I gave them the story as I am giving it to you now. But the movie will be the facts only. This book contains the facts as well as the spiritual life that surrounds them.

Dressing room encounters

This was a no-go zone. People could never understand that when they entered my dressing room after a show that I would react like a total stranger caught in the nude. 'But I just saw you naked,' they would say to the embarrassed covering-up 'stranger'. 'That was the show,' I would reply. 'Please leave now.'

When I look back and recall all these things they sure do not add up. I don't think there ever was or will be a person with my personality who would or could cause a total uproar and outcry in an entire country by removing her clothes.

Another rule I made was that I would never perform for individuals. There was safety in numbers. I set eight as the minimum number of people who had to be present.

Miraculous protection

I would have as many as five private shows in one night over the Christmas period. I could not drive and I did not have a car. The people who booked me had to fetch me. The first show would fetch me at home. The second show would fetch me at the venue of the first show. The third show had to fetch me at the venue of the second show and so on. The last show had to arrange to take me home. These were negotiations with people I had never met in my life and I would be paid by them to do a striptease show.

If you could have been a fly on the rear-view mirror of each car that transported me you would have said that this was not possible, taking into consideration that at every show the audience had consumed alcohol. The bachelor parties were the worst. At one show I arrived and found that everyone had passed out, except for my driver who was totally sober. I had a phone call the next day to ask if I had appeared. Only the driver was my witness that I had.

Never, not even once, did I have a driver who did not treat me like a lady. There was always utter respect and protectiveness.

I never doubt that this again was because of the prayers of my foster parents. I know that a spiritual presence must have been with me which caused the drivers to turn into protective angels. The power of prayer never ceases to amaze me. God, who is so faithful that even when we are unfaithful, He remains the same.

Prayers and curses

I know that there were more people who prayed for me. So strong was my influence on a country that churches had special prayer days to pray against the evil that I was bringing into their towns. Then there were people who condemned me to hell and then there were those who adored and admired me. The winners were those who prayed for my salvation and for Jesus to bring me into a personal relationship with Him. My foster parents never stopped loving me.

Their son, Erdi Baumbach, had a barrier that could not accept that any good could ever come out of someone like me and he refused for years to believe that Jesus had taken back his temple. It was only at Christmas 2009 that he phoned and said that he forgave me. That was the sweetest taste of the love of Jesus as a result of being forgiven by others. I am sure that forgiveness like that gives freedom to the giver and the forgiven.

I can't seem to separate the past from the present as I cannot help but see God's tapestry running through the entire life cloth.

The snake

Dead or alive, the show must go on.

You cannot have a relationship with a snake. People might like snakes but snakes will never like people. No snake is going to come slithering in haste, wagging anything in joy at the prospect of meeting with its owner.

With me and snakes the feeling was mutual. No affection lost between either of us. Unlike dogs or cats that crawl into 'love me' hearts. Snakes crawl into 'do not disturb' holes.

If fear of a snake is as bad as my fear of spiders then far be it from me to scare the life out of any paying audience. You might think I used some poor person in the audience as a hanger on which to hang my snake, but believe me, it was all pre-arranged.

If anyone expressed the desire to swap places with Oupa, the snake, I had bad news for them. Oupa snake had his five minutes of the forty-five minute show and only while I was still clad in at least a bikini (unlike the movie I made later, where I was nude). Then he was put back into the basket.

This one occasion was different. Oupa was the star.

The banners announcing our arrival in a small town in KwaZulu-Natal read: 'Oupa!!!' And somewhere in the small print it said I would be present too.

It was a barn dance. With Oupa as the main attraction there would be much less uproar from the community. A snake is a snake and a snake does as a snake does.

So what does a girl do when halfway to the venue, travelling from Johannesburg, the main attraction is lying dead in its basket on the back seat?

My sister Jean was driving me to the show. We exchanged a quick glance and knew that 'the show must go on'.

So that night I put in a performance for two. One dead and one alive. Fair is fair. You come to see a snake, you get to see a snake. We made a good team, the two of us. If one moves fast enough and the other is in the way, it gets taken along in the movement. So Oupa and Glenda Kemp moved as one. By the time Oupa was put back into the basket, no one was any the wiser.

If you had happened to stop along the road between Ladysmith and Johannesburg for a picnic the next day, and came across a very still python lying in the field, you would have had no reason to be disturbed. Dead snakes don't bite and dead snakes don't tell that two ladies had dropped him off along the way.

On another occasion before this dead snake experience, Jean and I were stopped by two traffic cops for going too fast. When the cops saw that it was Glenda Kemp they offered to escort us all the way to our destination. They had their police lights flashing and we went flying far over the speed limit until we reached our town. They asked for my autograph and went smile, smile, smile all the way home.

8

Scandals and court cases

Work; scandal; more work; more scandal. The time passed as if in a working dream. I was also getting to know my older brother, Dirk Kemp. He was the only boy born to my mom and dad. Dirk's marriage had failed and he moved in with us while his wings healed. I had never known my brother well until then. I stood amazed at this talented man. For one year he became my 'manager'. This was bliss. Not only did he now carry around lights and speakers and amplifiers, but he turned out to be the best compère a person could ever want. He had his own act. He had the audience in stitches and well prepared for my show.

We travelled throughout South Africa together.

Most of the time, I was oblivious to the headlines I left behind when leaving a town. But in this short time of dancing *Rapport* phoned me and told me I had been voted their 'Newsmaker of the Year'.

By now it seemed the entire police force, the army and the Dutch Reformed Church were out to get me. Dirk and I were like a Bonny and Clyde team, managing to stay one step ahead of the police until we got to Cape Town. It was very uneventful as the police said that I just had to sign an admission of guilt for public indecency, pay R20 and that was the end of the story. I paid my fine and went off to the next show. Somewhere along the line I signed another similar admission of guilt without blinking an eyelid.

Another case

This one was in La Lucia, Durban — a private house. The entire police force was there. I mean the entire police force must have been there, including the Special Branch. They all wanted to have a piece of the action. They surrounded the house in which I was performing. If I had been Samson I could not have fought my way through them. But I was not Samson and I had no intention of fighting anyone. I was an entertainer. I asked for permission to go to the toilet. The Special Branch man first investigated if there was any way of escape from that source. He even looked down the toilet bowl. Police were also planted under every window. I had no idea I had so much power in their eyes.

Once brought in to be charged, they had no clear idea of what to do with me, so they let me go. Huh?

There was confusion on my part and that of the police as we had no idea what the law actually stipulated. No one had ever done what I was doing in this country. My strips were at private parties so it was not regarded as public indecency. But somehow this could not be right. The law was out to get me. Some time or other I would put a foot wrong at a public venue.

And so I did.

A court case or a circus?

This happened in Pretoria on 5 December 1973. The venue was the Bon Accord Hotel, but they had closed the area off to the public and people were allowed in only by invitation.

Unbeknown to me, the happy fellows in the front row were the police. I went through my whole routine with bloomers and *Voortrekker kappie*, snake, oil, puppets and ended up wearing nothing but the oil lamp and then the strobe light. I dressed on stage and waved goodbye.

Not so fast lady! The cop introduced himself and told me this was the best show he had ever seen. The other cops also produced their cards as if this was some fan club and could not praise my performance enough. I was asked all the normal questions like 'What does the snake eat?' and 'Where do I keep the snake?' Not the normal procedure for taking in a criminal.

I was charged with public indecency. But this was the start of the most bizarre court case that ever hit South Africa. The press kept the whole of South Africa informed as they journeyed with me through the courts right up to the Supreme Court. There were astounding 'performances' from police who openly admitted to loving every minute of the show. Famous and highly-esteemed artists and performers stood up in court and professed to the show being artistic. My drama teacher turned up as a witness to my talents. The art form was so highly acclaimed that the magistrate's verdict on 1 July 1974 shocked the government and the churches: 'Not guilty!'

Glenda leaving the Pretoria Magistrate's Court with her attorney

Of course, this opened the door to other strippers, who were suddenly crawling out from under every stone.

The State appealed against the verdict in my case.

Everything that had previously been proved in court was overruled. I was found guilty and given a suspended sentence (20 July 1975).

After the court was adjourned for the last time the Judge walked down the aisle towards me. He smiled, shook my hand and said: 'I am sorry, I had no option. I had to find you guilty. I wish you success.'

We appealed. The conviction was cast in stone. Even the Supreme Court could not clear my guilty conviction. The only outcome of our appeal is that my name is written in the law books of South Africa. All law students will learn about the first strip case in SA history: State v Kemp.

These were the facts as they unfolded. But what no one knew was the total fear and loneliness that engulfed me as I saw myself spending years in jail. The endless cost of lawyers and arrangements, of having to repeat the identical show to prominent South African artists and performers. Professor Walter Battiss was among these. He was very impressed with my performance and my body and asked me to pose for him for a painting. He and his wife fetched me and took me to their farm in the Pretoria area. There I was lying in the nude while this artist worked away in silence. The final result: a landscape! That was so special to me. This man could look at a woman's body and turn it into hills and valleys. He donated one of his modern works to me but unfortunately I lost it in one of my house moves.

Going to jail was a very real possibility! Even when the final judgment was made and the sentence read that I was to spend three years in jail. My heart stopped. Then it was suspended. This would, of course, mean straight to jail with the next offence.

What any normal woman in my situation would have done is surely to have stopped right there and then. But no, not I. The show must go on!

The next court case — stripped to the bone

The police were now losing the plot. They were like little kids taking sweets from shops as if there was no law and order.

My cheeky announcement must have unsettled them: 'I am going to strip to the bone.' The venue was public and licensed. So I kept my promise and stripped to the bone. Where is their sense of humour? The body stocking I wore was thick and black and the bones that were sewn on to them were thin and white. Under the ultraviolet light only the bones were visible as the clothing fell aside. Before the last notes of the music faded I was surrounded by policemen and taken away to the charge office. Bones and all. The person in charge agreed with the shocking behaviour of our police force. The obvious alcohol he had consumed made him miss the point. He could not tell a bone from a stocking. He ordered me thrown into the cell for the night. Then I was to appear in court the next morning.

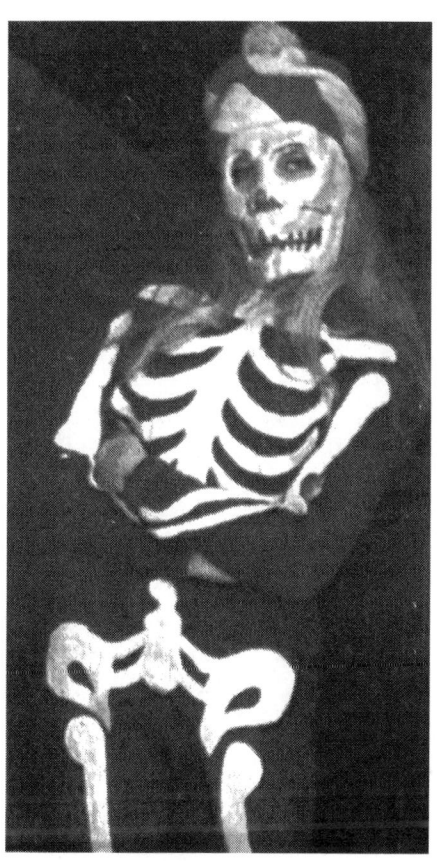

Stripped to the bone

I then knew what it means when someone says, 'The bottom fell out of my world'. My whole being turned into a sob. I was innocent in this case. I had as much power as a newborn black baby in the South Africa of the seventies. Walking to the gallows could not be worse.

The policeman answering the instruction to take me away was at my side and leading me towards the cells. Did he feel the sad fear come through my arm where he was gently touching me or did my foster parents' prayers set in again?

As if he were Batman, my guardian angel intervened just in time. The officer, leading me by the elbow on the way to the cells, took a wrong turn. We ducked and dived the James Bond way and he ended up with the 'merchandise' under the protection of him and his wife at their friendly little flat somewhere in civilian life. I was given a mug of hot chocolate and tucked into bed by this godly couple. Early the next morning the policeman manoeuvred me into court to make my appearance without anyone suspecting that I had not seen the inside of the cells.

The case was thrown out. There was no case! Is anybody held accountable for unjust arrests? How my heart bled for the black people of South Africa. I pray that they also had the opportunity to experience the kindness of godly people along the way.

Apartheid

I never did understand the Afrikaners' apartheid laws. And once I got to know Jesus I knew that apartheid was an abomination to Him. It was hard to read anything in the Word without it being clear. Surely a child could tell that this nation was being blinded.

What is the most precious thing to a nation?

Its children!

Who did people leave their children with when they went out pursuing a career and freedom? With black ladies. Yet they did not call them ladies. They had a derogatory name for them. They left their most precious 'possessions' with someone that was so low that they were not even allowed to sit on the same bench or under the same roof in the house in which they worshipped the Creator of the universe.

Whose bosom did their babies nuzzle up to? Who could dry their babies' tears but was not allowed to drink from the same cup as them or their household?

Then the baby grows up and falls in love with that which represented his first caring love — a black lady! Now he finds himself in prison for wishing to continue what his parents had started.

The moral censorship laws I could accept although they frustrated me as I felt I did not fall under any category. I still had so much dance energy inside of me and so little 'space' in which to do it.

The authorities and I were standing in total opposition to each other.

Black dancer on whites-only stage

I turned up at a much-publicized show painted pitch black from head to toe, and wearing an African wig. Was I trying to be different or was I making a statement?

Drums. Just drums beating as the black figure moved in slow motion, balancing a basket on her head.

First the silence. Then, in Afrikaans, a shrill voice of a woman rose up above the sounds of the drums and the silence: *'Dis dan 'n swart k***** meid!'* (English translation: 'This is a black woman'; using a derogatory term.)

Mission accomplished?

It started in a town called Volksrust. A group of people booked me to perform a cabaret act at a public venue. Then Volksrust was divided and a small war broke out 'for' and 'against' Glenda Kemp. Then the war spread like wildfire and the whole country was drawn onto the battlefield and I was in the line of fire!

Glenda painted black

I said I would shock them. The publicity was so intense and the reactions from all sides of the country so strong that I had to do something that was up to their expectations. I would do more than that.

Everyone expected me to sign my own death warrant and to strip naked. No one expected me to change my identity and dance my way into the apartheid laws. Some way into the show I pulled off the afro wig and my long blonde hair crowning and flowing around the black face and body made the whole scene more bizarre.

Like a Colombo of old, I was going around kicking up dust and, as it settled, another town was put on the map.

Glenda Kemp - Snake Dancer

9

Karl Koczwara

The Bible says to look forward and to leave the past behind. Now if I want to go back into the past to make myself miserable all over again, then that is okay; it is my problem. But I will not go back and bring up things from other living people's pasts and cause them misery. It is not my business to remember what I think others did to me. Jesus is not going to come back and throw my past in front of me so I am not going to bring out all the painful memories which we both might have. My marriage to Karl Koczwara failed and as divorce goes, it was very painful. But God has made something beautiful out of all the broken pieces. What use would it have been if I had gained the whole world and had lost my soul? I have my soul and eternity is still ahead. What is the past but for us to use it to God's glory?

In those dancing years, Karl was the only man in my life.

I had no idea how he felt about the stories of my stripping that covered the front pages week after week. He never cared if people came over for my autograph or asked questions. The only time that I know of that he did see me dance, was at the first two discotheques and he laughed it off as the *Dying Swan.*

My work schedule was hectic and we never saw much of each other.

Safaris

Later when I stopped dancing I became a chef on Karl's safaris to Botswana. There were funny incidents with monkeys peeing on the food and rubbing my toothbrush in the mud after the rest of the party had left on game drives. And the lion that killed a buck next to where we were sleeping on the top of the Land Rover. Not to mention when Karl unhooked the trailer and dropped me off to protect it against lions and elephants. Only once they had left and I was standing alone in the wild, did Karl and I realize that this could be suicide, if not murder. Thank God no lions challenged me.

An elephant once did. I was preparing food for 15 clients. The garlic, onions and tomatoes (all hundred of them), were all cut up and neatly prepared to go into the pot. It was at this stage that an enormous elephant decided to look me in the eye whilst putting one foot in front of the other in my direction. To the onlooker it was obvious that we were an uneven match. One of us was at a disadvantage. The elephant's trunk was touching my table. I leaned forward over the camping table throwing my body as protection over the smelly garlic and onions. I looked the elephant in the eye and told him in no uncertain terms that if he dared to touch my ingredients he would regret ever having met me. I really did. The elephant turned around and walked away.

Karl recently reminded me of our single-engined boat that lost its motor in the bottom of the swamps just before sunset. That was when I developed a great respect for the dugout *makoro* boats that glide along at the slow pace of a hand movement, but they do get there.

I also remembered when Karl rescued a big bird that managed to get entangled in something in a high tree. He surprised me at the dedication he showed towards helping this one bird in distress. It was a happy moment when Karl and the bird descended from the tree, bruised but free.

Why anyone would pay money to be all shook up in an old Land Rover and live on a cup of water a day and be imprisoned in the heat of a car, is beyond my understanding. During the entire safari the tourists would complain and suffer and when we got back to Johannesburg they would rave about the wonderful holiday. Working as 'chef' demanded hard work and lots of planning. Buying and packing happened long before each trip. Why did I do it? Is this not what a woman does for her man?

The fact that I was pregnant at that time was not the reason for our marriage. Kimmie was fully planned. I know that it was the third month of me being off the pill. This is the most incredible happening in my life and it belongs to another chapter.

At Christmastime each year Karl gave Kimmie the experience of a wonderland Christmas tree and a Hansel and Gretel gingerbread house that arrived from Germany and which the two of them would assemble. Later my sister Joan's family was included as well, and they received their very own house which they could take home and build. Easter was also celebrated in an unforgettable German style with hunts for eggs.

It was Karl who made it possible for Kim to study Speech Therapy at the University College of London. He is very good to her and there is nothing he would not do for her today. They have their own special father-daughter relationship and she spends a lot of time and holidays with him.

Today Karl and I are friends and I love him with the love of the Lord. He is the father of my child and that is the most precious thing between us. Whatever happened later, we had shared our youth in each other's presence and that alone is a sweet memory.

My prayer for Karl is that Jesus will touch him and for the first time he will pour his heart out to Someone who loves him as he has never been loved before.

'... God our Savior, who wants everyone to be saved and to understand the truth. For there is only one God and one Mediator who can reconcile God and humanity – the man Christ Jesus' (1 Timothy 2:3–5).

The big house with the big dance room

It was time to move my bed out of the garage in Parkmore and into my own bedroom. Operation 'Big Move'.

We found the house. I would have needed two biscuit tins full of money for this house, but by that time I was familiar with a bank account.

Even now, when thinking about this house in Observatory it is like looking at a past that I held in my hand and reluctantly handed over to God. When the judgement fire has had its share I don't think any of my tears and laughter will remain. Everything was so important then. The shows, the alterations, the sisters, the marriage, the birth, the betrayal, the divorce. So many years all in one sentence. All that remains and always will remain are the good family relationships. These we should cherish above all else.

Nothing of this was known the first night we slept in our big house. My sister Jean and I just lay there on the floor in the empty house and promised each other that this was the house in which we would all grow old. At that time we did not know that we could throw the dice but that God decides the number. All of us were 'little children' choosing our rooms and spots. This time I got the best room. They were all best rooms but this one had wall-to-wall mirrors and so much space.

The real reason for choosing this house in Observatory was the downstairs basement that just was waiting for me to turn it into my own dance theatre. Many bachelor parties were to be held here.

My brother left to start a new life with a new wife and I was back to being picked up from show to show by strangers in strange cars.

I decorated the walls with pictures from girlie magazines and centre spreads. I installed special lighting and put the place to good use. The walls don't have to tell tales of what happened there as I have first-hand experience and can speak for myself.

You probably expect to hear about these low-class sleazy clients who found their way through the underground to turn up at Glenda Kemp's venue. Not so. Doctors, surgeons, businessmen, government officials and show business people. (I remember doing a show for Des and Dawn Lindbergh and their guests.) I never did a show that did not result in another show. The same people came back over and over again.

Snakebite

The gentlemen arrived with the normal nervous schoolboy giggling atmosphere that accompanied them. I was always there with my farm girl nature to welcome them and make them feel at home, before the other

Glenda Kemp returned to entertain them with the show. When one of the men informed me that he had to leave as he had never been in close proximity to a snake without something bad happening to him, I laughed it off as a joke.

Oupa, the snake, was not the star of the show and his lazy nature did not make him much of a dancing partner. I did not think he had the energy or the intelligence to strike or to find a place to aim at. I did my usual dance around the basket, opened the lid and dramatized the contents of the basket by moving away again. The snake's nature is to slowly move out the basket once the lid is off and to go from object to object. I would stand in front of the basket imitating snake movements. Oupa followed his instincts by finding my leg and then slithered up to my tummy and proceeded to my face. Then it happened! I had the snake's upper teeth stuck in my eyebrows and its bottom teeth stuck under and into my top lip. The snake had struck and caught me in the face. His teeth were stuck and he could not retract them. I held the snake's heavy body in my hand so as not to have the weight tear my face. I went out of the room and pulled his jaws apart and got the teeth out of my flesh. As the jaws closed the snake's teeth cut a clear slit down my nose. I stopped the bleeding and returned to continue the show. I had a very silent audience.

My face, and in particular my lip, had swollen to three times their normal size. On looking into the mirror I knew I needed a doctor. The first doctor I dialled was in the middle of his dinner and he was not going to fall for a snakebite interruption joke. The other doctors were not available. My sister drove me to the hospital where I got an anti-tetanus injection and some antibiotics. It was only a few days later that the newspapers got hold of the story and came to take a picture. Even then I looked like a prize boxer who had lost a fight. My eye was black and my lip still swollen.

Big bang no man

Another 'not-so-happy' story the walls could tell you if I kept silent.

The men forming the bachelor party were more excited than usual and taking in every move in total wonder. Everything went well and I carried them along from moment to moment. I enjoyed dancing as much as they enjoyed looking and responding with faces that could tell no lies. When the last number faded and I blew the end of the show kisses with my hands, the one gentleman went from his sitting position on the floor, into throwing his body up into the air with his hands outstretched, shouting with glee, only to be silenced by the low ceiling connecting with his head. He was literally knocked out!!

Was this a dead body? Do you phone the ambulance? Do you phone the police? What do you tell the bride-to-be? By the time the ambulance arrived the injured man was making strange noises but the smile on his face was unchanged. I heard the next day that he was fine.

10

Glenda movie — 'Snake Dancer'

I was busy watching *Haas Das* on South Africa's new television transmission, when Dirk de Villiers knocked on my door. Dirk was a well-known movie producer and director. He thought that my life story should be captured in a movie. I was 29 years old and here was a man wanting to make a movie of my life.

It would be a full length feature movie for international release and would have the title *Snake Dancer*. Dirk came armed with a scrapbook that told of incidents that were larger than my life. Dirk and I discussed the various headlines which had been recorded in the tabloids.

Needle in a haystack

I knew this was not good when I felt a sharp pain in my foot. The needle I had been sewing with a moment before was missing. I knew exactly where it had gone. After jumping around and pinching my face into a ball I ventured to look. Was it a good or a bad thing that half the needle was lying on the floor? As for the foot, only a red entry mark was visible.

The needle had broken off in my foot and the doctors had to remove it. Why this was not just a local anaesthetic and a quick removal of the needle I could not tell. I was booked into hospital and received bills from so many doctors you would have thought the needle was a national health threat. The doctors' geography was also in question as they were wondering about my birthmark that was located nowhere near the needle area.

Even stepping on a needle had a way of becoming a topic for household discussion. Newspapers! Read all about it.

Kemp v Kemp

Talk about newspapers. I wish I had kept the clipping about this tea party. If I had, I would have copied it out word for word as it had covered a double-page spread of *Rapport*, the Sunday paper.

A Dutch Reformed Church minister had spoken out about my doings and this was causing ripples. The interesting part was that the poor man had the same surname as me — Kemp. The newspapers could not let this pass by without making something of it. So whether the minister invited me of his own accord or whether the press instigated it, I can't remember. But Kemp invited Kemp for tea. The good and the bad were sitting at one table and drinking tea from the same teapot.

Every word we spoke was recorded in print and played back to the country. We both were able to get into each other's 'shoes' and we agreed to disagree on points we did not agree on. Either way, Kemp came out tops.

Singing snakes! And now the movie!

A record company had just used my name and my pictures to make a Glenda record (singing and laughing about snakes; a Government school teacher and a Sunday School teacher). I was well established in the country's history book. It was very much, 'braaivleis, rugby, sunny skies and … Glenda Kemp!' (Words quoted from a car commercial of the time.)

With the noose of the law tightening around the freedom to see my shows, Dirk thought people would flock to the cinema to see the notorious stripper in action. Dirk wanted to climb onto the Glenda bandwagon as it seemed to have a formula that was working.

This was a dream come true for me. From a very young age I had wanted to be a movie star. Never did I dream I would be the star in my own movie of my own life. I could not wait for the cameras to start rolling. My co-stars were all well-known South African actors. This was something that very few people experience.

My dancing was captured forever. So were a few other things that would come back to bite me in the ankle. This movie brought truth to the saying: 'Your past will catch up with you.'

I had no control and was left to the mercy of the camera. The shows were the same but the camera was going where no audience was allowed to go. No lighting effects or wall behind me to shield my body from the eye of the beholder.

A scene from the movie 'Snake Dancer'

Of course there was an overseas version including the nudity and a South African version. I never did see the 'overseas' version and thought what the eye didn't see wouldn't hurt the heart. Now that this 'overseas' version is floating around on DSTV I feel I would like to sneak into each household and hide the remotes.

Dirk de Villiers was developing wandering hands that I found myself fighting off in most of my free time. He did not know much about me. Or maybe he was not used to women turning down the advances of a film producer. Luckily for me he did get the message and found himself a girlfriend to see to his needs. Big relief. I could relax and concentrate on the work ahead.

And work it was. I had no idea how hard it was to star in a movie. We were busy from before sunrise to after sunset. The worst was the time spent sitting around waiting. There were make-up artists (I never usually wore make-up except if I was doing a modelling job), clothes fittings, lines to be learnt, and lots more waiting.

Meanwhile my sisters were finding their feet in new relationships and were moving out of the house to start new lives. I invited the movie crew to move into the vacant rooms. So the scene around me was very busy both on and off set.

The movie came at the right time for me as the suspended jail sentence was too close to home. During the last show that I held in the basement dance floor, my sister came running in, shouting for me to get dressed. The police were invading my home. It was time for me to put a plug on my energies and to look for new pastures. Besides acting, my heart was with children and teaching. The movie gave me a break from watching my back and allowed me to concentrate on doing something for which no one was going to arrest me.

If you think the promotional side of the movie was any girl's dream then you don't know this girl. There were designers' dresses to be fitted, and smiles and signatures to be handed out at opening performances, which were not my cup of tea. Anything that resembles the artificial is to be avoided.

The movie was not what Dirk De Villiers had hoped for. South Africans were not flocking to see a family-rated movie on Glenda Kemp. They wanted the excitement and adventure of secret agents sneaking around incognito to watch what was not allowed, in places where no one saw and seeing what no one dared to see. The movie did not provide that. It would also have been politically incorrect to publicly show an interest in someone who represented forbidden fruit. Then there was the ending, where the hero arrives on the rescue scene only once the life had been squeezed out of his beloved by his rival, the serpent. I bet, to the government's delight.

11

New beginnings

So with Glenda Kemp dead in the movie I thought of rising from the ashes and becoming what I had intended to be in the first place: a teacher. Children, here I come.

I thought it was a good sign when the Head of the Teachers' Training College agreed to an appointment to meet with me. I entered his office with big smiles from both of us. He seated me down and listened intently to my plea of wanting to complete my diploma and wanting my name cleared.

Then he opened a drawer in his desk and pulled out a big book that looked like something very important and official. He opened the hard cover and to my surprise I recognized from the upside down position the cuttings staring at him. Just for good measure he turned the book around so that I could see my sins as recorded in the book of the Teachers' Training College of South Africa. I wondered who had taken the trouble to cut out every detail of my doings and then to stick them neatly in order in this black book. It must have been in anticipation of just this moment to share it with me. There was even an instruction from the Minister of Education to block the way for me should I have the audacity to try to re-enter the pastures I had left.

I think this was the time I had my first cigarette.

That was that. My next approach was to the Epworth Children's Home in Germiston. Here I was warmly welcomed and the door was opened as only someone who knows Jesus can do. I was employed as a Relief Housemother for the various houses where children are placed as families. I lived in a flat above the home and rented out the big house at Grace Road.

There was some fun and games to be had by all as I went out of my way to treat the children with love and to spoil them with treats on my relief weekends with them.

Loss of a teaching job as recorded by 'Scope' magazine

House burnt down

This was such a short diversion from dancing before the headlines interfered. It was nothing I had done. This time it was what was done to my house. It burnt down. I was taken there and stood in the house looking up at the sky. A very sad moment. This is it?

I was lonely.

Karl was there; but Karl was not there.

His only comment on the tear or two caused by the situation was for me not to be such a drama queen.

As I was so involved in all the negotiations with the insurance company regarding the rebuilding of the house, I left the Children's Home and waited for my life to take direction. The direction came just as the last parts of the house were rebuilt and decorated.

Madeira

I don't remember where this offer came from, but before I knew it I had a return air ticket in my hands and was booked to perform at a restaurant/night club in Madeira. It was just across the road from the Sheraton Hotel. I was older and much more mature than when I had ventured to America. I knew and had stipulated what my duties were as an entertainer and that there were no other motives attached. A new door opened. For once I could do my show without wondering if every face in the audience was a policeman with a warrant for a three-year jail sentence in his pocket.

I had my sights set on another venue. I had heard of Paul Raymond in London and that his theatres were reputable and professional in an honourable way. Raymond's Revue Bar in London was high on my list.

My ticket to Portugal was via London so I arranged to meet with Paul Raymond and to audition during my one-night stopover.

My experience on my London stopover was reason enough to make me allergic to travel. I found myself being interrogated in a little room and having to answer the same questions over and over again. The fact that it was a one-night stopover made the authorities very suspicious and they were certain I was smuggling drugs.

About drugs

If they had known just how little I knew about drugs they would have allowed their babies to escort me wherever I wanted to go. Later in London when my naivety was no secret anymore, Paul Raymond jokingly said that I did not even know what 'coke' was and that I probably thought it was a drink. This time I thought I would show that I was not that ignorant and said I knew what the other coke was; we use it at our *braais* in South Africa in place of coal.

The wonderful thing is that no one ever tried to change my lack of knowledge of drugs and they chose to keep such information away from me in a protective way. In another instance I was asked if I had a 'button' for someone and was rather prepared to cut off the very top button of my shirt to give to the person in need. They had no words to describe my ignorance.

The only time I touched marijuana was to pass it hastily on to the next person in the circle before removing myself from its presence.

Cold snakes and warm tears

By the time the London authorities let me go I had another problem. I was not going to share this with them. Which gate catered for the arrival of snakes? I decided to get my luggage first. I stared at the moving luggage on the carousel knowing I would recognize mine by some garment that would be half hanging out of the suitcase. It was a joke among my sisters when they were not around to pack for me. Being organized was not one of my gifts. Then I saw it; the upside-down basket, moving at the same pace as all the normal passengers' luggage, making its way towards me. If the snake had spent the night in the hold with the luggage, we were in for a frozen audition.

By the time I found a taxi, I had not found myself yet. The tears ran freely as I packed myself and my drapes into the surprised cab driver's back seat. The only word we both understood was 'Paul Raymond'. And I had been told that they spoke English in London. And they had told him we spoke English in South Africa. When the taxi driver pointed to the snake I was determined not to break the language code between us. I had an audition to be done and I did not need any more enemies. I needed a job.

London stopover deal

Paul Raymond and his anchor team were bowled over by my performance and I was given a signed six-month contract. I was the only girl who was doing her own act as Paul Raymond's team had their own choreographers and props. To my delight they did not think the snake was necessary in the show. I was paid a higher rate than any other girl and allowed to perform without make-up or painted nails. The standard for perfection was very high and the girls had to keep their slates clean. The environment was safe. The stage door could have been in South Africa, so far removed was it from the theatre's entrance. There was no contact allowed with patrons. This was a place after my own heart.

My performances were so well received that I was still there two years later. These theatres usually never keep ladies longer than three months as their patrons like variety, so everyone is usually always on the move.

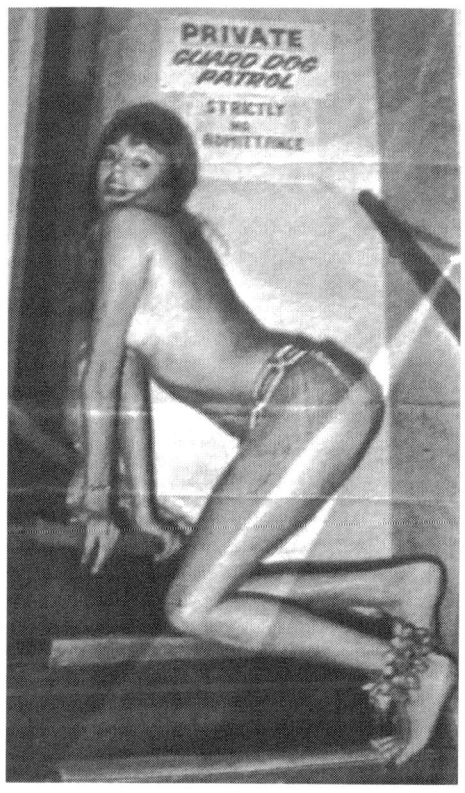

Backstage door of Raymond's Revue Bar

Portugal

The picture of Madeira that I paint for you is one of endearment. This is a place where you go for a climb and not a walk. The deep sea lets you enter without restraint from big waves.

The word negative did not enter into this experience. Visits to wine farms to do my shows were all positive. The only enemy that followed me like a ghost was loneliness. And even this was dispelled when my sister Linda and her husband James came to visit me. We travelled about the town speaking and singing Afrikaans songs. We behaved like little children at a party, doing our traditional Afrikaner dances in the streets and behaving with a freedom that everyone endorsed. The harbour had put its spell on me. I climbed up an area overlooking the sea and was back in the tree on the farm with all its enchantment.

My summer clothes went with Linda on her flight back home to South Africa while my winter clothes and I went back to conquer London.

London — West End theatre

Raymond's Revue Bar and the Windmill Theatre

I was met by a limo at Heathrow airport. I travelled in style to the offices of Paul Raymond. My experience with Paul Raymond and his manner towards

In a newspaper report, Soho star Glenda says, 'I'm so happy here.'

me allows me to speak only with respect for the man. He understood the problem of accommodation and pointed me in the right direction. Of course, he was not there on the street corners to point me to anywhere as for some time I had no idea where I was going to or coming from. The London Underground removed any sense of direction that might have been left. But I survived and was always in time for work.

Paul Raymond arranged for me to stay in a more expensive flat for a month while I looked for something more permanent for myself. The landlady at the expensive flat tried to take me for a ride when I left by saying I had blown a hole in the bathroom ceiling next to the geyser and so she could not return my deposit. She obviously used this hole to keep all the foreigners' deposits. But she was in for a surprise. I knew a bit about the housing law. So I told her that she could keep my deposit but I was not leaving that flat and I would not pay rent in future. (Of course I would not do that, now would I?) I knew that she could not throw me out at all. She was very surprised to see my determination. I had even told Paul Raymond that I wouldn't be in for the shows as I was 'squatting' in the flat. The lady got such a fright that she immediately gave me back my deposit.

Then I shared a flat with a girl in Holland Park for about a month before finding a flat in Soho. The girl I shared with was very strange. She definitely took drugs.

My first day at work

Do you know what hit me in the face when I walked into the big dressing room as one of many nude performers? The nudity! Nude girls everywhere; painting their nails, packing their things, searching in their bags, putting on make-up. They wore no clothes! They moved around with the ease of being in a public coffee shop without a thought about having private parts on their bodies. Do I make sense? No, I guess not. Is it not worse to be nude in public on a stage? I know, I won't argue with that. I somehow had this stupid notion that if you were acting a part it was not wrong.

This was a proper theatre. Everything was very professional. Every girl had her own chair and a mirror surrounded by lights. A whole crew of stagehands was running around backstage changing props and warning girls to get ready. They would have conversations with nude girls as if they worked for the emperor's new clothing company. There were professional full-time choreographers and lighting people employed. No cost was spared to portray the nude girls in fantasy worlds.

Then there was me. No make-up. My only prop was a baby bath with a white soapy vest in the water. I would start off by stomping my foot to the African beat and then have the whole of Africa break through me in a dance routine that made everyone sit up in surprise and wonder. I was most nude when clothed in a wet clinging garment. The words, the rhythm and the enjoyment would spill over to the audience like the water in the baby bath. They enjoyed it so much that they wanted more even when the show was over. So I heard that many people came back again and again to experience a bit of Africa with a white skin.

I say heard, because I could not see. The theatre's spotlight blinded the performers into an isolated world of activity. This got to me. I missed my little 'stages' where encouragement could be found in the faces of my beholders. I missed that childlike admiration that let me know that I was doing what I set out to do. Dancing to a blinding spotlight has a way of dehumanizing the experience.

Illness and God's angels

Colin, our backstage manager, was a big teddy bear of a man. This man was to make an impression on me that has lasted a lifetime. He had a wife and a little son called Zack.

I became ill.

I became very ill.

I was aware that there were people taking care of me and when I was able to focus, I noticed things that belonged in a little boy's room. Colin and his wife had taken me into their tiny London flat and put me in their son's bedroom. His wife had nursed me day and night until I was well enough to take care of myself. This woman did not know me from a bar of soap. There was nothing in it for her. I keep coming back to my foster mother's prayers and the angels whom God sends to minister to my needs whenever I am going into a downward spiral.

Friendships

I tried to cross the barriers by baking some cookies from *Cook and Enjoy for Beginners*. Considering my poor domesticity record at Swartruggens, where I did Magriet Bischoff's English homework and she did my Domestic Science, then maybe this was the wrong route to use to try seal a friendship. Besides providing a bit of sweetness, the cookies did not help any foreigner to speak English or to renew their short-term contracts. The once or twice I joined the girls in a night out it involved some drugs and at that stage I would go home. There were some routes down which I was not prepared to travel.

Walking the streets of London in my underwear

Midwinter outside. Warm heaters inside. Single lady cleaning her flat in her underwear. With a 'la la la' in my song, a dustpan in my hand and a broom in the other, the cleaning was continuing in a matter-of-fact way. Nothing to write home about. That is until I opened the door to place the dustpan just under the doorstep where it could catch the dirt without spilling it. I went down on my haunches behind the scoop, away from the door. Such a simple everyday task. Then the slam of the door.

Suddenly the figure on the outside of the door is not so ordinary any more. The song on my lips stopped. I knew that door. It was shut. I also knew where my key was; it was on the other side of that shut door. So if I know all this why do I push and pull with all my might and groan and moan as if I had a friend on the other side who would hear and open up for me? Face the facts my girl; you are in your underwear, locked out of your flat with a scoop and a broom and the snow outside.

The one thing you don't do when you move to a new country is familiarize yourself with where the local locksmiths are. Many things go through your mind but only one thing is practical. Tell your legs to move and to take you out where there is information to get you inside again. I did that. I did not see the point of taking the broom and the scoop with me. I was about to be embarrassed and no broom or scoop was going to make it any better or any worse.

I must have been shivering but I don't remember that. I just remember standing outside my building in Brewer Street in the middle of Soho and waiting for a crowd to gather around me laughing and pointing. Nothing happened. This is London. This is Soho. You wanna run around in your underwear; then run around in your underwear. Here you have to be weird to be normal.

I stopped someone: 'Please could you tell me if there is a locksmith somewhere nearby?' His eyes locked into mine and never wandered once while he explained the way to the nearest locksmith.

Needless to say, I was very happy to see the locksmith. He and I must have made an odd picture walking down the road towards my flat. The door was opened and the case was shut.

Loneliness

If loneliness were a relationship then we would have gotten married in London. It clung to me like a toddler to its mother in a dark place. My working hours, my work and my personality were in a head-on collision with relationships from the outside world.

I think there was a song that said loneliness is a mist that wraps itself around you. I can relate to that. The longer the hours, the thicker the mist. In the daytime people were working and in the night-time people were sleeping.

Entrance to my flat in Brewer Street

I now lived in a bachelor flat in Brewer Street. Nobody lives in Brewer Street, but I lived in Brewer Street. The daily market set itself up under my window at four o'clock in the morning. After much moving and transport trouble this flat fell into my lap. I walked across the street to work.

The area was a sex bazaar. Even the innocent market had a sexual feel about it. The hungry eyes that turn anything into a sin paraded there. I moved in total isolation, being in the core of the corruption but walking out, as if on water, where none of it could touch me. My intimate friends were the theatre, the cinema and books. My enemy was food. Both were in abundance. To protect myself from food I would not have a crumb in the flat. If something makes you stumble; cut it off. Too much time and so little sleep and so homesick!

There was one lifeline that kept me hanging in there. It came in the form of an envelope which was dropped through a slit in my door. My mother's letters! I knew the postman's time. I would position myself in front of the door so as not to miss any second of the thrill of hearing the footsteps approach, pause, the sound of paper, and then, its last step in a long journey from South Africa, the letter came popping through my door. For good measure I would first look at it and then hold it and then read the front and back, before opening the envelope. I lapped up every bit of news. I missed my mother and my sisters and brothers really badly.

Desperate loneliness called for desperate measures. I found a place where not even loneliness would want to be seen. A peep show! Very much like the slit that let my mother's mail fall at my feet but instead of 'mail' it is the eye of the 'male' that feeds coins, allowing the slot to remain open while the 'lady' on the other side removes her clothes. A bit like being in the *Big Brother* house, but this was the 'big bad big brother'.

Women who work in these boxes have as much life in them as the contents of a coffin. You can sit and read a book or have a cup of tea until you hear the click of *Big Brother* announcing his presence. Then you could continue reading as long as you removed something with the turn of each page. Not me. If I wanted to be bored I would stay in the flat. So there I was, dancing for my life, having eyes without bodies observing me, that fed money into a contraption that kept me in their view.

One evil always leads to another. With my adrenalin racing as it was, I needed help to sleep through the activities of the early morning market. Sleeping pills! They had to be stronger than the human body's desire to be awake during the day and the ears that told the brain about the noise happening outside. So the doctor prescribed strong ones. So strong that even when I was awake, I was still asleep. I needed something to energize me for the evening's dancing ahead. Diet tablets were just the thing. They did a double job. Kept me away from food and gave me stamina. Did I say earlier I had nothing to do with drugs? Who was I fooling? I thank God that this was only for a short period of time and through circumstances I was brought back to sanity.

The Windmill Theatre also belonged to Paul Raymond. I was now working at both theatres. Between doing my schoolgirl act there and the bath act at the Revue Bar and the peep shows, something was bound to give in. It was my hamstring. I thought I could fight through the pain and do what a dancer had to do. But the body is sometimes much wiser than the brain.

The first thing my body threw out was the peep show. Then it made me betray the music by sending the beat on ahead and I never followed. Backbends, splits and bending all resigned and the only thing left that worked was a smile. No one in Soho pays to see a smile.

Paul Raymond was not ready to release me. I was sent home for a holiday and to be recharged with my family's love. My mother was at the airport with her *frikkadels* and *vetkoek*. My sisters and my brother Dale were there with happiness that competed with mine on our seeing each other again.

Karl was there, but Karl was not there. He had visited me only once in London.

I did go back to London to finish off my contract, in a state of holding my breath and only letting it out once I was back on home soil where I could kiss the ground. There is no place like home!

What happened to the snake?

If 'hissstory' serves me right, Oupa Python exchanged his African heritage for a British passport.

Hopefully, he would have lived and have known the likes of slithering under the leadership of Harold Wilson, tasted the iron of Margaret Thatcher and witnessed the inauguration of John Major. That is if he did not squeeze the life out of the wrong object, and if he lived to a ripe old snake age of 25. What the British do with departed snakes is anyone's guess. A bag? Shoes? Not.

He did not broaden his horizon outside of the English countryside as his papers were all that returned to South Africa with me. There was no investigation as to the whereabouts of the owner that did not accompany his documents.

Our 'divorce' papers were signed when Paul Raymond of Raymond's Revue Bar declared that he wanted my show, but not the snake. I was not cruel, as the relationship between me and the snake was purely a business arrangement wherein the snake served as a logo and nothing more. I was happy to have cleared the notion that a snake was my claim to fame. I did have a show you know!

So what did happen to the snake? I left it behind in a happy state with a line of voluptuous dancers bidding for the use of its services. The decision was left to the owner of the girlie enterprise. I danced off into the English limelight, solo for the first time and enjoyed the 'hiss-less' ride.

Even today, after so long, the first question asked by those who remember those years is: 'What happened to the snake?' Now you know!

12

Is there life after dancing?

Delta Safaris (1980)

Glenda Kemp, South Africa's notorious snake-swinging stripper is marching into the Botswana bush, to the sound of the children's song: *Ek is 'n dapper muis* — the brave mouse that was not afraid of anything. But, what about spiders? Spiders? Well besides spiders, I am not afraid of anything. But what about … leaving home? Long journeys in a car? Cooking? Wild animals running free? Using the bush as a toilet? Going without bathing?

'Help, what am I doing here?'

I know the answer to that question: 'For the love of a boyfriend.' A woman in love is like a drunk man; you can't reason with either of them.

Shaking knees

The first time my knees shook involuntarily was the first night I slept in the bush in Botswana. Sleeping in the open, on the top of the Land Rover.

My vocabulary does not include describing the sounds that emerge when a lioness makes her kill on a helpless buck. The word 'terrifying' sure does describe what was going on inside of me and the buck. This is not like sounds from afar, or a close-up on the television. This is darkness. The encounter between the two animals was directly next to our car.

With hindsight it was a blessing that the buck was around or else we might never have made it into the safe interior of the Land Rover.

Run baby run

This was the second time I discovered that my knees could actually shake without my having any control over them. It would have been cool if it was a freak show competition, but it was a lion outside my tent and I could smell his breath.

The haunting sound from afar made my hair stand on end; now that it was accompanied by the smell of his breath, I wondered how much protection the thin canvas of the tent provided.

I would have run to the Land Rover but, except for the movement of my knees, I was frozen.

A month before this I had been on a stage, applauded by admirers. Now, here I was listed as 'stripper's delight' on a lion's menu, served with shaky knees and the aroma of fear.

Somebody do something.

My memory does not serve me well as to who ran first, Karl or me. (I am sure I was waiting for his instructions), but when we dived into the Land Rover the rest of the paying clients were already piled up inside. A speechless bunch we were, but we were alive!

Botswana intruder

When we got to a place where we slept in a bed with a roof over our heads it was pure luxury. The lodge was not the kind with five stars but it did have running water and you could submerge yourself in a bath. You also could sit down at a table (after days of 'scraping' food out the fire), and be served food from a kitchen.

So then what is the highlight of this story? The occupant that shared a room with me! For non-paying guests you would think they would keep a lower profile than to get to the intimate point of reading my book as along with me. I do not take kindly to surprises and did not do so then either.

The bed under me was bliss and the blanket over me was cosily pulled up with my arms sticking out to hold the book that was resting on my chest. My knees were pulled up. A serene scene.

You know that feeling when someone is looking at you? I had that feeling. In spite of being very involved in whatever I was reading, a sense of uneasiness came over me. I did not have far to look. In fact it was far too near. It was as close as my pulled-up knees. It was just above the book. (If it was that close, how come I am still here to tell the story?)

My eyes had stopped reading even though they looked as if they were still in focus on the storyline. I decided I would count up to three and then look up; with my eyes only, so as to not alert whoever or whatever was giving me this uneasy feeling that I was being observed. So I looked up.

Four eyes met at arm's length. It was intense. There, peering over my book was the biggest rat I had ever seen! A big, fat, hairy rat breathing into my face. Amazing how long a person can stay frozen in a moment before defensive action sets in.

They heard my screams all over the camp, both the people and the animals in the vicinity. They were the screams of an endangered species. They were my screams.

By the time the 'rescue' team stopped me from running; the ammunition and firearms were already aimed in the direction of my room. There was no lion or snake or escaped madman. Only a crumpled blanket had reached the far side of the room with a moving object sandwiched inside it. The movements in that blanket were strong, but not enough to warrant the use of firearms.

Why people made such a small thing of a big, fat rat is beyond me. We are all entitled to our opinions.

A hairy story

Oh the adventures of a bush safari! Nothing like a good mug of campfire coffee! Savour every sip as you gaze into the secret language of the campfire; dressed in its glow as if by a protective garment against the wildlife watching in the dark bushes around you. A feeling as safe and warm as the coffee caressing your throat.

Then, as suddenly as a lion making its leap, the peace is disrupted. The coffee in your mouth turns to needles and a wild beast from inside seems to have you by the throat. Poisoned coffee? Help seemed as near as the nearest doctor or hospital which was not near at all. Even trying not to swallow was like trying not to breathe. The needles persisted in their attack on wherever the coffee had touched. It was anybody's guess as to who had done it? The first clue was to shine a torch down my throat. For the second clue, shine a torch into the empty coffee cup.

And there was the culprit! A hairy caterpillar without its hair. That was the closest I ever will get to a caterpillar again. Sharing hot coffee and prickly hair. Sounds like a visit to the wrong hairdresser. I survived. The caterpillar? Sorry, it did not make it.

A friend and ally

There was one breath of fresh air that blew into the safaris. This came in the form of a client from Germany, who stayed on as the wife of Karl's partner, Manfred.

Yes, Brigitte and I were allies and together we coped with the monkeys, the elephants and the food. Blessed again with a 'forever friend'. Brigitte remembers this in an email she sent to me in January 2012, which I have quoted here:

'My dear friend

We actually did just one trip together and that was my first trip to South Africa. The ones before we didn't know each other and afterwards it was me who took over the work you did and then after all that you fell pregnant with Kimmie.

I have attached two very typical pictures which confirm the notes I found in my travel diary. The few pictures I made were in black and white. All the others are slides and I don't know how to copy them. And now I quote those parts of my diary in which you are mentioned.

The day I first met my dear friend Glenda was on Tuesday 12th August 1980 at 7am in the middle of Jo'burg. (I can hardly believe that it was almost exactly 32 years ago.)

A quiet, slim, long-haired, blonde woman who accompanied us on the trip to Botswana.

She was Karl's girlfriend and responsible for many future 'heerlike' bush meals.

As the pictures show, Glenda was either busy in the kitchen which was most of the time an open fireplace und only twice solid built kitchen units or as the second picture reveals waiting patiently in the dust and hot sun or cold mornings of Botswana. She never complained or was even upset. The only time she really got cross was because of the baboons.

She spoke Afrikaans and English, but only a few words of German. Glenda joined Manfred a lot and later me and two of the guests who spoke English. She really liked to have a good laugh and it was in the middle of nowhere, somewhere in the vast Bush of Botswana when I first heard her typical giggle! (She still giggles in the old way.)

For our first dinner Glenda prepared steak, garlic bread and potatoes which she wrapped in tinfoil and placed them in the open fire. Delicious! Next morning at 6.45 am and a freezing -4 degrees, it was like magic as Glenda produced roast chicken legs, hot coffee and cookies for everybody. Eventually we arrived in Maun and carried on to Crocodile Camp our base camp for the next four days. First night in the swamps!

Glenda, Karl and Manfred had trouble with the motorboat and only arrived at the place where we were supposed to spend the night at 10.00 pm. Without Glenda around dinner was a solemn occasion. We opened the only food we had ... three tins of goulash that we heated in a pot over the fire and stirred the soup with a branch of a tree. Next day, the cook was back (thank God), and we had lovely tuna salad in the heat of midday. Sadly, we soon came to our last evening in Maun but Glenda was too tired to join us at bar for a last drink.

Monday. That night I helped Glenda preparing the meal and we talked a lot.

Tuesday. Moremi Game reserve, Campsite near a bridge. After dinner Glenda wanted to be a bit on her own and walked down to the bridge. Seconds later she hastily returned and called: "Karl, there is a lion on the bridge." We all held our breath, Manfred stayed with us and Karl cautiously went check. It turned out to be a hyena. Shame! We all relaxed and everyone went to see Glenda's 'spotted lion'. Later she told me that since a recent accident where a lion attacked people she was scared of lions.

Wednesday. I got a big fright because of an attacking elephant and stayed at the campsite in the tranquil company of Glenda. Later that afternoon while we were away on our game drive she had lots of trouble with baboons.

23rd August 1980

Chobe game reserve. It was late afternoon when I noticed a baboon right in front of the car and told Glenda who looked up from peeling potatoes and realized that four of them were already sitting in the car. During our entire stay at Chobe, Glenda was only able to cook if somebody was on guard and kept the baboons at bay. That evening I had a fabulous talk with Glenda.

Arriving at Victoria Falls we were far too busy looking around and enjoying the scenery, so only Glenda really relished the luxury of solid built huts, showers servants who took care of the dishes and for the first time she had a day off.

Kiss and hug from Brigitte

Mit freundlichen Grüßen

Brigitte'

Scrap metals

After a stint in Botswana as safari cook with Karl, the most natural thing for me to do was to gravitate towards one of my sisters. Joanie to the rescue. Joan and her husband had moved from being salary earners at the bank to being independent earners in the scrap metal business.

My first reaction was: You must be joking. Metals. Drums full of metals. Dust and oil and dismantled parts. I still had not learnt to drive a car and now I had learn to distinguish between copper and brass.

If ever anyone wanted a patient and good teacher they would find one in Joan. She managed to teach me without pulling her hair out, or laughing in my face. And there I was, with my very own scrap metal shop; taking two buses in the early hours of the morning and clocking in to the hardest boss I ever had — me. Hard work and long hours are guaranteed to bring in the bread and butter.

If Joan had not dragged me to the licensing department on pretence of renewing a shop licence and then putting me in a learner's licence queue, I would still be walking. I finally got a driver's licence at the age of 32. First I conquered the world and then I got my driver's licence.

Kim's birth

I got much more than that. I got Kimmie! Not much bigger than a speck of precious metal at the time, she would come along and change my life. Life had just begun.

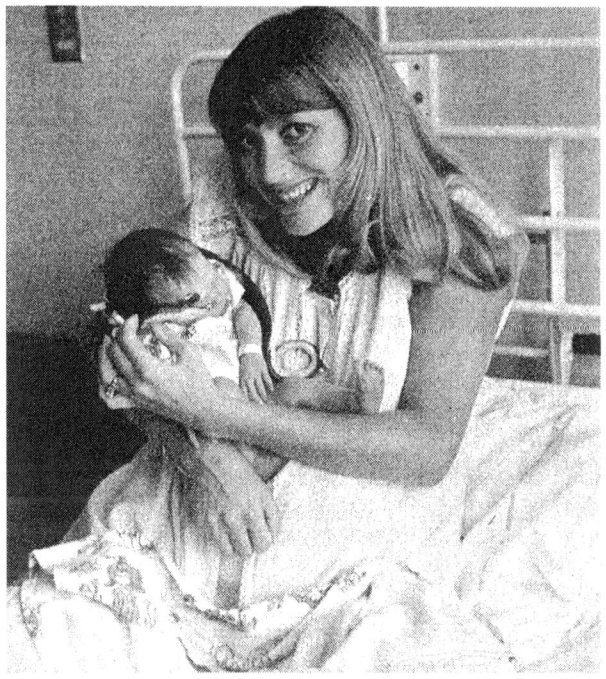

Glenda with newborn Kimmie

Karl and I had moved into the big house in Observatory.

I had looked at the mental list we had made years before with ten kids on it, comparing it with the desperate list which was now on the wall, with 32 written on it. Not 32 kids but 32 years. Karl and I decided to settle for the last list and threw the pill out the window and waited.

Living by our own standards, we had said that marriage would only follow on a full term pregnancy.

Karl joined me in the scrap metal shop. Kimmie, growing in my tummy and in my heart, filled the big space between me and the steering wheel and the world was a good place to be in.

I was ecstatic. I was pregnant. Nothing, but nothing prepared me for this. For the first time in my life I truly loved. She was growing nails and hair and body parts while living inside of me. I looked at baby clothes that would soon be on her little body. For once I was speechless.

The lady writing the script for the 2011 movie asked for details about Kim's birth. Of course I told Kim about the request and by writing to her I had the information for the movie and more for the book. Here is an extract from my letter to Kim:

> *'I did not really describe the wedding in detail in the book and I did not give a detailed account about your birth; about the Peter Sellers movie I watched when my first contractions came and how your dad and I went to the hospital in the rain with the windscreen wipers doing all the talking all the way there. Then when the nurse told me it was almost over, only five more hours to go, I thought it might as well have been another year.'*

As for me, I lived my second childhood through Kimmie. I know all mothers love their children but I have never done things the way all others do them. When Kimmie was born and put in front of my head I licked her little body. I felt like a cat with a kitten. The love I held in my heart was reacting with such joy.

My home was filled with children. I was determined that she would have friends and not grow up alone.

Boutique

I never thought I would see myself in a boutique, but I should have known better than to say never. It happened. My neighbour Elvera and I became great friends. When a successful dressmaking couple crossed her path she wanted to draw me in to be part of the new boutique.

All I wanted was to be a mother. They twisted my arm as we had employed someone else and it did not require too much of my time. That was another venture that surprised even me.

Teacher's diploma

I now applied successfully to complete my teacher's diploma and started teaching at the same time that Kimmie started school.

When I saw that she was having trouble with her times tables I worked out a method of stories and rhymes to help her memorize them.

I could write a book about my only child. The umbilical cord between a mother and a child is never broken.

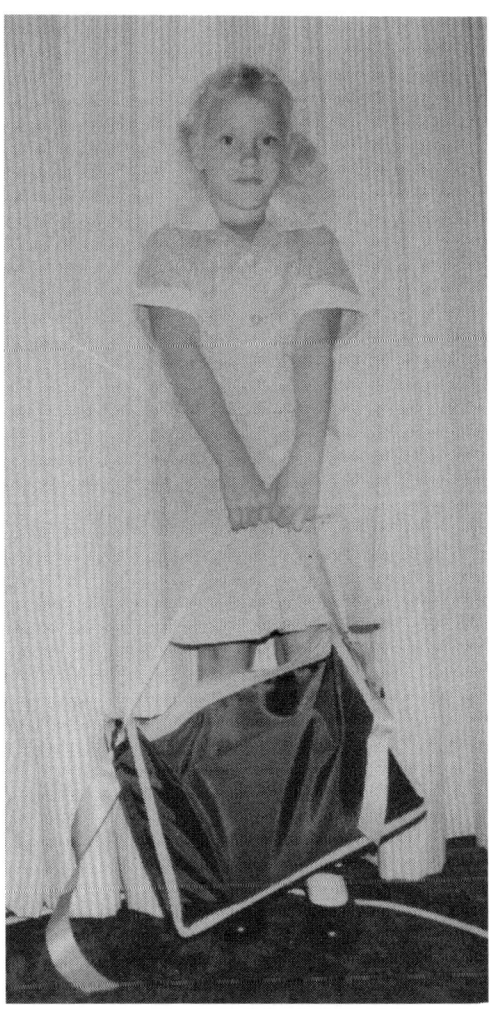

Kimmie in Grade One

13

Durban

End of a marriage

My marriage was over. My sister Jean put my mother, Kimmie, our dog and me, onto the train to Durban while she stayed behind to do the packing and sorting out. Sister to the rescue — again.

Durban — first years

The beach is the only witness to my sorrow. My weeping reached high tide for the pain of a failed marriage. Only those who have been there can decipher the code. Worse still is watching the scars of divorce being engraved on your child. I would use my womb as a childproof helmet against the crashes of life. But God made us to walk upwards and onwards even if the spirit is crippled.

My sister Jean, my mother, Kim and I became a family. I was the breadwinner. Jean ran everything like a pro. My mother socialized and collected friends. My sister Linda lived around the corner and my sister-in-law Gerta (my brother Dirk's first wife), around the other corner. We ran an open house.

My sanctuary was God, the beach and my tears.

I started teaching at Bushlands School where my presence always brought forth a Glenda Kemp joke from the headmaster. I don't think he ever realized who I was and I did not tell him.

Loving children is not a good enough reason to be a teacher. Being organized and being a disciplinarian are. I was neither of the last two. With the gaps in my elementary education, not being able to spell became a source of embarrassment. The demands made by red tape were endless. All I wanted was to work with the kids. So I stopped after some time and concentrated on being there for Kimmie. I could survive on the income from the house in Johannesburg.

Kimmie steered her love and life into horses. To support her in this interest meant endless trips to the stables and back. Her new found friend Nicolette (Nikki) and the dog were as much part of our life as the air on the Bluff. Kimmie and Nikki were best friends for years. Nikki's mother Eliza Robinson and I were later to become soulmates beyond what we ever imagined. Eliza was diagnosed with cancer. Her health deteriorated and then she slowly recovered from her cancer treatment. Nikki moved in with us for a time during her mother's illness.

Puppet shows

Do activities find me or do I find them? Suddenly Kimmie, Nikki and I were entertaining children at birthday parties with puppet shows and fun and games. Kimmie dressed up as a mouse, Nikki was the bear and I was the clown. We advertised and travelled all over Durban on weekends. This is another colourful insert in my life that provided its own challenges.

Somehow the years went by.

Kimmie became a teenager. It was the teenage years that brought me to the end of my resources. I realized that there comes a time when however much I waved my wand, the Red Sea would not open.

The God I was talking to on the beach was an outlet for inner me's. I had no relationship with Him. He never talked back because I did not let Him.

If there is one thing I would die for, it is my child. But looking at the failure of my contribution, my life would serve no purpose just as my worldly love was doing more harm than good.

Then I remembered who did die and whose blood had power. I went back into that tent of the orphanage time, and asked God to save my child from all evil. Drug abuse, the all-evil monster that devours our children, was lurking around the corner. Kim had not taken any but the people entering her life were wolves in sheep's clothing. My child was my business and I made it my business to know what was happening.

God had already provided my lifeline in the form of Eliza, who had left me an invitation to attend a Bible Study. The invitation just hung there. They had a prayer list. Any needs I wanted to put onto their prayer list were welcomed.

I had a need. Eliza took my request for Kimmie and the ladies prayed.

Saturday was disco night at the local school. I smelt a rat! Eliza prayed. I phoned Karl, Kim's dad, and asked him to be in Durban that Saturday evening before the disco started.

Karl parked his car in a dark spot under a tree. I dropped Kim and her two friends as usual and they waved me goodbye. My car disappeared out of sight. Karl kept the girls in sight from the darkness. They stood for as long as it took for my car to disappear and then proceeded to climb into a car with some young adult males who, I had been told, lured young people into drugs. What happened then would forever be written in Kim's diary. Her dad (who Kim thought was in Johannesburg), opened the car door and asked her where she thought she was going.

This was my first adventure with Jesus. I wanted more of Him. I joined Eliza's Bible Study.

Bible Study

This was so weird. The women were all about my age or slightly older than me, but somehow I only saw a bunch of old ladies with big smiles as I entered the circle for the first time. My feet were still full of sea sand and my hair was wet from the waves. I was the fish out of water. But they were the fishermen. Things started happening.

The first half hour consisted of Christian songs that bored and irritated me. This was easy to sidestep as I timed myself to arrive at subsequent meetings once the songs came to an end. Later these same songs walked with me wherever I went. The day I realized that they were prayers it became a heart matter. I learnt every one of them off by heart and stored them there.

We had Bible Study homework. I had to look for a Bible. There was one somewhere in the house.

Enter God

The first thing this merciful God gave me was an intense hunger and thirst to know Him. I stood with open mouth, in wonder, at what I was reading in his Word. I realized the wasted years of filling myself with the world and vowed to make up for it.

My teachers were Bevy Vermeulen (my Bible Study leader), and Cecile Burger from Radio Pulpit. Bevy and her husband Ampie would send me home with homework and be on call 24/7 and I recorded Cecil Burger's *Into the Sunshine* and *Word a Wenner* programmes on tape. Having been a bad sleeper all my life I now found valuable material to fill my wakeful nights with. I played and replayed Cecile's words. She taught me a very valuable lesson in my Christian walk: the Bible. Read it and read it and read it, and write. Cecile never said anything without substantiating it with a Word from God's Book. God actually spoke into my situation with whatever I was reading that day. This is a pattern which developed over the next 14 years.

I have more than 60 diaries in which my continued conversations with God are recorded. Conversations that make me eat his Words and live them, while He moulds and loves me into his future.

When I say God, I mean the God of Abraham, Isaac and Jacob. He is the only true God who gave us His Son Jesus Christ to unite us with Him and who sent us his Holy Spirit to walk with us and teach us and connect us.

'Now the rest of the acts of ..., and the many oracles about him, indeed they are written in the annals of the book of kings.' This is said in the books of Kings and Chronicles about many of the Old Testament kings as they came to the end of their lives.

I am no king or queen but I am the adopted daughter of the King of the universe. The rest of my life is recorded in my diaries as intimately and openly as they were conceived and received through my life with Jesus.

God's answer … 30 years later

When I was 15 and still in the orphanage I wrote to my future foster mother and I drew a picture of a water jug with stones in the bottom of it. I told her that I had Jesus in me but that He had never reached the bottom of my soul.

Tapestry hanging in my church

It was as if He was on the surface but did not reach the foundation. Thirty years later when I sat in our church and looked at a tapestry showing a jug pouring out water, representing the Holy Spirit, I got the answer to that question. The reason God did not reach deep down was because I was not pouring out. I was reading and praying but I never told others about Him or shared Him with anyone — like a river that stagnates and then becomes silted up.

The second time I went back to Jesus I started a youth group and began telling those who wanted to know, as well as those who did not want to know, the Holy Spirit filled me all the way to the foundation. I find it awesome how God gave the answer to a question I had pondered over so many years before. That tapestry is still hanging in our church. God explains things in different ways to each person as we are so unique in our relationship with Him and yet so similar. He is just as alive today as He was when He opened the Red Sea and as alive as He was in Jesus when Jesus walked the earth.

My new journey in marriage to Peter Harper started off with such a jerk that we both fell off the bus. Only by obeying the Word, and by seeking continued intimacy with Jesus, are we now on track and picking the fruit of endurance and forgiveness.

I look at Kimmie and I boast in my weakness as only God's strength and mercy has brought her to where she is today. I had my inner struggles of trying to do what was best for my child when my own foundation was still under restoration. Meaning well, but doing badly and sighing in relief because of God's safety net underneath her.

I experienced that airport farewell that many a South African mother knows about. I felt as if I should have run after her and pinned her to the ground and taken her back home.

I cupped my hands in prayer and literally filled them with tears. There goes my Joseph, into the pit, to be sold to the enemy, to be grown up through trials so she can stand in the Kingdom and know that God had meant it for good. Step by step and prayer by prayer, her London life is recorded in my diaries. My thanks to her friend Yolande, who even after getting married to Paul, allowed Kim to live with them while she finished her degree.

Memories of my mother (died 3 May 2005)

My mother lived with me for 18 years of her life. She had Alzheimer's disease. The final years of caring for her while she was ill were so hurtful and difficult that it is extremely hard for me to write about them. Looking after her caused me an incredible amount of pain but it would be unfair to speak about the negative things she did when they were due to her illness.

The people making a movie about my life just sent me an SABC documentary that was made 13 years ago, called *Dancing with Snakes*. Suddenly it was as if my mother, who had passed away five years previously, was sitting in my lounge telling the story of the widow who gave her kids to the orphanage because her husband had died and she had no means of caring for them. The cold clouds that altered my mood, I thought, were caused by the regret of having allowed them to film me in the nude with the snake.

The emotions from the last four years I spent with her came back in an unfair portrayal of her that is too painful to recall. I should rather remember her letters that kept me going in the orphanage and while I was in London, the lovely meals she made for us and the never-ending dishes she washed. She even kept my letters. Every letter I wrote from London.

An extract from my letter to Kimmie, on my letters to my mother from London.

'As you know, the letters were there in the "attic". I read all afternoon and hardly made a dent in the pile. There were even two from Portugal. It amazes me to read about the daily happenings that I had totally forgotten. In the beginning I had some friends but they were really wacko and their boyfriends or husbands were always beating them up. I can see why I kept to myself once they had moved on to the next countries. No one had a contract for more than three months. Only me, for two years.

The overall feeling I get is "What a waste of time". How we chase wind and air all our lives. I won't even read all those letters. I really can see that God's plan for us is the true plan. Even with all the calamities in our lives there is always that sense of a purpose and of being on the way to eternity.

Do you know what I wrote in my one letter? (I had only been there a short while.) I wrote that there was a minister from the church who came round to the dressing rooms and talked to the girls, just letting them know he was there if they needed him. All these nude women and he talks and sits as if he is doing a normal house visit. He wished me happiness in my job at the theatre. I could not believe it at the time and I find it strange that I had forgotten it. I don't know what to think of him. He obviously did not come back again.'

Youth Group — (First one 1997)

> … that Christ Jesus came into the world to save sinners, of
> whom I am chief. However, for this reason I obtained
> mercy, that in me first Jesus Christ might show all
> longsuffering as a pattern to those who are going to believe
> on Him for everlasting life.
>
> – 1 TIMOTHY 1:15–16 (NKJV)

Meeting Jesus is not an experience you can keep to yourself. Your seeing and your doing are forever changed. You see people and know what God can see and what God can do. The light of God had moved into my life and I was not going to put it under a bushel. Because Kimmie was the front-page person in my life it was only natural that God's influence on me would flow over onto the youth. Kim and her four friends formed an intimate group to hear how Jesus' Word was unfolding in my daily life. Before long the extended dining room table was too small. Word spread around that muffins and cool drink were being served while Jesus was being preached.

This was also the time when Peter Harper entered my life. We attended the Alpha course together and he dedicated his life to the Lord. Everything we talked about and did and breathed was Jesus. My foster mother had told me that the man you can pray with is the man you can marry. So I became Mrs Glenda Harper in 1999.

14

The enemy's table

Where there's smoke, there's fire

The only fire that was near this smoker was the fire of the Holy Spirit. Don't turn your nose up in disagreement. I came to Jesus just as I was. I smoked like a chimney all over the Holy Book. God had things to do with me and He was not going to start with taking cigarettes out of my mouth. His business with me was that I should get to know Him. When my vision became blurry I simply wiped the ash off the Bible with a stroke of my hand. That is how God and I spent our first months in each other's company.

Let me explain it to you this way: Find a table near you. If there is not a lot of stuff on it, then imagine stuff on it. Now when you give your life to God, you hand over that table as it is. If you wait to first clean up your life beforehand, you are lost, because only God can do that.

So would God come with a big arm and wipe everything off that table with one stroke and let you watch it crash to the floor? Not so.

God has one word for you — Love. For God so loved the world ... God loves you! And in the same breath, you must love the Lord your God with all you are and all you have. Now how can you love someone you don't know?

So your first job is to get to read your Bible and to fellowship with other family of Christ so that you can get to know your new 'spouse'.

Back to the table with the stuff on it. Now God had no finger pointing to my smoking on that table for a long time. But when He did, it confronted me in every reading, sermon, radio talk and in whatever type of reminder there could be.

Every smoker wants to stop smoking, without God telling them to do so. I was no different. One time I managed to give up smoking for a whole three hours (and one hour was taken up by the church sermon so it should not count). Every Monday was 'giving-up time' and every Tuesday was 'shame for failure' time. Oh these little white things had themselves superglued to me like a skin.

Walking hand-in-hand with God did not make it any easier. For some people it is a different story. Bev from my Bible Study woke up one day and 'wham'; the desire for smoking was gone. She never craved again and never smoked again and never gave it a thought. Nothing works like that for me. My road is always hard and difficult. The nearer God's finger pointed to the cigarettes on the crowded table the more it became an obsession with me to stop smoking. The greater the obsession to stop became, so the demolishing effect of failure grew in me as well. Satan told me I should rather leave God as I was not walking in his power. Never; who would I go to? I'd rather be a smoker sitting with my God than a smoker sitting with Satan. That is about it; you have those two choices. God is a merciful God and knows my heart's desire.

Nothing goes to waste when God is at work. I started having a heart-rending understanding for the drug addicts I was coming across.

'Lord, if it is this hard for me to stop smoking; how hard is it for them to stop drugging?'

When you pray where you are touched, you pray double-edged sword words. When it comes to dealing with people struggling with addiction, there is not a hair of pride on my head. I come in humility and with the knowledge that only by the grace of God have I come through this one day. Gluttony falls under the same category.

'Lord is there one disorder I did not pick up somewhere along the way? How privileged I am, for there is so much more to be thankful for and so much more reason to be dependent on the One who created me.'

'Therefore let him who thinks he stands take heed lest he fall' (1 Cor 10:12, NKJV).

'But let him who glories glory in this, That he understands and knows Me, That I am the LORD exercising lovingkindness …' (Jer 9:24, NKJV).

'And the Lord said, 'Simon, Simon! Indeed, Satan has asked for you, that he may sift you as wheat. But I have prayed for you, that your faith should not fail; and when you have returned to Me, strengthen your brethren' (Luke 22:31–32, NKJV).

Then God hit me where it hurt! Kimmie. My cigarettes were disappearing faster than I could smoke them. Kimmie was disappearing more often than was her home-loving nature.

Two plus two makes four.

Then one day our smoke columns met. I caught her red-handed. Now here was the pot calling the kettle black.

'I will stop, Mom, if you will.'

If you witness more failures than you can count, then you are very safe to back that horse to lose the race for you. Kimmie was convinced that her mom had her limits, and giving up smoking was one of them.

The pain began.

Peter was in it with me. He had to fight the years, having started smoking at the age of 15. I only started smoking in my late twenties or early thirties, but boy, had I made up for the years I'd 'deprived' my lungs of nicotine.

The first step is to remove all temptations from you. (Have you ever tried doing this with food?) Every possible place a cigarette could be found had to be snuffed out and destroyed. It was the biggest 'search and destroy' operation I ever ventured on. And rightfully so.

The time came when I turned into a bag lady and unashamedly rummaged through our rubbish bins looking for the hope of a one puff on a *stompie*.

The whole world teamed up against me to start me smoking again. At every trial the enemy stood with a white sin held out to me and a promise that this would make me feel much better. I walked around repeating victory Bible verses like a woman at war.

Then God allowed me a dummy. It must have been after banging my head on the wall that I grabbed the nearest cylindrical-shaped object that represented a cigarette. It was a yellow Bic pen. I took it in a smoker's grip and brought it to my mouth. I sucked long and hard and held my breath in my lungs. Then I breathed out with a big sigh of relief. This helped.

This was ridiculous but it worked. Soon all who knew me got accustomed to me and my yellow pen-sucking. The cravings lasted for a very long time but with longer breaks in between as time went by. I was resigned to sucking at my pen for the rest of my life. But it did stop. One day I was without the pen and I cannot remember how or when. So here I am, a non-smoker with every bit of sympathy for all smokers.

The taxman

When God pointed his finger to the taxman at the table of sin, I pretended not to see it. If I had been the woman at the well I would have talked about the different places of worship and avoided the issue.

The Word of God leaves no doubt about this topic.

'Give to Caesar what belongs to Caesar, and give to God what belongs to God' (Matt 22:21).

'Pay your taxes, too …' (Rom 13:6).

'Everyone must submit to governing authorities. For all authority comes from God, and those in positions of authority have been placed there by God' (Rom 13:1).

My dog shivers and shakes when there is thunder and lightning. The Receiver of Revenue (now SARS) did the same thing to me.

At that stage I had a house in Johannesburg which I was letting. The unpaid electricity bills left by the tenants were almost more than the income, but still it was an income.

I went to my church and told on God. God wants me to pay my taxes and I have no idea where to start. Did the church have anyone who could help me?

They put me on to Marian, a lovely, young, talented lady who was doing the church finances as well as being the church musician.

When she saw my unbelievably disorganized form of 'bookkeeping' she must have thought she had bitten off more than she could chew. (I should have stayed with my biscuit tin, as it made more sense to me.)

I realized the impossible task ahead and decided to hand myself over to the Receiver of Revenue. I said goodbye to my family and loved ones and prepared myself to accept the consequences of my tax sins.

Finally, I stood before one of the Receiver's officials. I told the truth and nothing but the truth. Somehow she must have ignored my error and seen the effect of hours of prayer, praise and worship. She smiled and said it was not a problem. I could start paying taxes as from that year.

Ever since then I have been a regular taxpayer. Another blank spot on the enemy's table.

I grew in great spurts through trials that came in like waves, each one more fearsome than the previous one. I was the eagle's baby who was thrown out the nest to learn to fly. I remember crying out to God that He was giving me stones when I asked for bread. I thought of David and Goliath and realized the disaster it would have been if David had been given a piece of bread instead of a stone. There is a time for a stone and a time for bread.

I was a full member of the Bluff Methodist Church but my ministry was wherever I set my foot. When I started a second-hand shop down the road from my house, Jesus took over and met with every customer and wrote their names into his Book of Life. The children of the area found a place to eat of his bread and drink from his juice as they came in to be helped with homework or just to stop for a chat.

15

The first stone

Prologue

I wasn't going to write about these negatives. It is a fact that dwelling on negatives is a no-no. They happen; we learn from them; we grow closer to God; we forgive and we move on. The reason I am including them in this book is because so many people have left the church as a result of being hurt. There is no church where you won't be hurt and there is no church where you won't be hurting others. Fact. We need fellowship. We need each other. I walk and work intimately with the people I will be describing here as the ones who caused the hurt. The chances are they won't even know that they are the people I am writing about. The good they have done in my life so overshadows the hurt that it would have been my loss if I had changed churches at the time.

The most important thing God has taught me, that has helped me through many hurts, is that nothing can happen to me that does not first go through God's filter. Satan had to ask God's permission to do things to Job. The person I need to be to fit into God's plan has to be sifted by these experiences. If there is one thing God hates, it is pride. Every hurt has shown me that there is still too much of me, and too little of Jesus. It is not about me. It is about Jesus. It is about praying and loving those who hurt you.

'I appeal to you, dear brothers and sisters, by the authority of our Lord Jesus Christ, to live in harmony with each other. Let there be no divisions in the church. Rather be of one mind, united in thought and purpose' (1 Cor 1:10).

'… Why not just accept the injustice and leave it at that? Why not let yourselves be cheated?' (1 Cor 6:7).

My church cannot save me and your church cannot save you. This is because no church died for us. No pope, no bishop, no pastor, no evangelist can save us, because none of them died for us. But here is the name of the one who did die for us. It is JESUS! JESUS! JESUS! Only Jesus saves!
                                                  REINHARD BONNKE

A suicide — 1998

She hanged herself from the rafters of her garage ceiling. She hung there by her neck until she was dead.

And I had been there only two days earlier.

They said I was the wrong woman to have gone there. 'They', being my church minister and leaders. They said she had asked by name for a certain leader to go, but she had not gone.

It was God who took me there. I was sitting at the little table in our kitchen minding God's business in the Bible when the Holy Spirit came over me and told me to go to this woman. I only knew her from two meetings at the Alpha course and all I knew was that she lived near the police station. Nothing else.

It was God. He told me to go. I immediately got my car keys and went to the car. Satan was also there. I know because my car would not start.

God said to me to go. It was raining. So I took my dog on the leash and started 'going'. It was a long walk.

I was in the Spirit all the way. Our father who art in heaven was my Father inside my heart and under the soles of my feet.

I reached the police station. Without stopping I prayed to my Daddy to show me where to go. I had no street name and I had no house number. I turned left after passing the police station. I walked to where the road ran dead and stood still. Me and my dog, wet in the rain. I just stood and looked at the only house on the right.

Then she came out. She did not say anything. I did not say anything. She hesitated and then came closer. We looked at each other.

'Are you Glenda Kemp?' she asked.

'Yes, and God sent me to come and tell you that He loves you very much.'

'I saw the documentary movie on you. They said you were living in Durban.'

'Yes, and I love Jesus now. And He personally sent me to come and see you. He even brought me to your house.'

She told me at that stage that she did not usually let anyone into her house, but she was so happy to meet the real Glenda Kemp. She let me in.

The house was immaculate. I was wet and out of place. She told me that she was not that perfect, it was actually her husband. He was in the army and everything had to be immaculate. She told me he did not love her.

The front of the house opened up to the wide ocean. All this beauty for the eye but the heart was empty.

She brought out her photo albums. She opened them to me. I cried with her over the sadness of the child she had loved and lost — who had committed suicide. I cried with her over the sadness of her husband who was unfaithful to her. We cried together and Jesus was there in all his perfect love embracing the situation and revealing his plan. I saw inside the albums. I saw inside that which she was prepared to show me but she did not reveal the plan for the rafters in the garage. But Jesus knew every detail. He spoke to her through my mouth. He did not want her to do it but she had a choice. 'Choose you this day whom you will serve.' My overwhelming message from God was that He loved her. That there was hope.

She hugged me when I left. She seemed so fine.

God took me there. He did it.

Two days later she was dead. She committed suicide.

I still cry when I think of this.

I did not understand. I threw myself before God and cried out with all that I had. I remember the turmoil inside. God, did I fail you? Oh God, I am so sorry.

Mother Theresa said God did not call us to be successful but to be faithful.

I was faithful.

When I came down the steps at the church and heard the ministers and two other leaders talking in a resentful way about the wrong woman having gone who should not have gone, and the one that should have gone but did not go, I listened.

I was God's woman and God sent me. God will never ever, ever send the wrong woman.

I was the right woman.

> *Why is God using some people and not others? Imagine you have two stoves at home, one hot and one cold, and you want to make yourself a cup of coffee; which of the two would you use? THE HOT ONE. Don't pray "use me Lord", but "Lord, make me useable". His fire makes us useable. The useable He uses automatically!*
>
> *REINHARD BONNKE*

The time when the church said I was the right woman

There was an awkward situation at church. A self-confessed prostitute had walked into the church and asked for help. The welfare had removed her children and she wanted them back.

The church was at a loss as to how to treat the situation.

Guess who came to mind? Glenda.

I was thrilled to be given my first assignment by my church. I know that all assignments come from God. I feasted on a meal of prayers about the situation before parking my glory *tjorrie* in front of the assigned house.

'Yes, what do you want?'

Believe me, this was not a friendly voice. This was not the person I had to see either. This woman with the aggressive manner and loud voice was about my age. Not young at all.

'I am Glenda from the Methodist Church. A lady came to ask for help and gave this address.'

She then used the name of my Father, but she was not praying.

' … You are Glenda Kemp!!! I've been a big fan of yours for years. Come inside! I saw your documentary the other day. I can't believe it is you.'

She told me that she chases any church members away as she hates hypocrites. For once I was welcome and I don't think it was a compliment: or was it?

I felt the love of God for Florence from the first moment I walked into her cluttered house. She cleared the things off a table and offered me something to drink. The lady who had asked for help was her daughter. Listening to this dear woman was like watching three different movies at once — a horror film, a love story and an action movie — all on fast forward. It took all of five years for her to screen all these movies for my perusal and for me to slap the Word of God in there with every pause it took for her to take a new breath.

Yes, for the next five years Flo and I met every single Saturday without exception. Every Saturday she made the most delicious tart and provided juice. I brought the Bible and shared the experiences I'd had with a living God that week. We had the most unusual, amazing relationship. Even my Alzheimer mother and my sisters were dragged along from time to time as I was never going to miss our Saturday Bible Study. Flo is a rough diamond and Jesus loves her.

Everything has its season. Flo accepted it when I told her the season had come to an end. God was moving me on.

Kicked out and 'escorted' to my car by bouncers

From the heading you might think I am getting my chapters mixed up and this chapter belongs to the past.

Not so. The venue was an evangelistic revival tent put up on the Bluff. My crime? I prayed with one of the youths who was struggling with drug addiction.

It was I who invited them to the tent meeting, praying for God to move through his revival Spirit which I believed dwelled in these meetings. This young man and his girlfriend, together with Kim and her friend, were the reason for the start of a youth group at my house, that was to flourish until the children passed through their school walk and into the world.

On my way to the big tent I was as excited as a child going to the circus. The thought of meeting with Spirit-filled Christians with Jesus as our focus point always has this effect. I am so keen for God to write on my blank pages. I wondered if I was lit up, as the glow of the Spirit's expectation surely must show. I waited for the arrival of my young couple and then the beginning of the sermon. When I was told that the young man could not come in as the evil one was preventing him; I went outside and told him to kneel. I prayed for God to enter him and set him free. That is when a crowd made up of the tent preachers and organizers surrounded me and asked what I thought I was doing.

I was dumbstruck.

'I am praying for this young man,' I said.

'We know who you are,' one of the organizers or pastors told me. 'You work for the devil.'

Dear God, this can't be happening. (I still cry when talking about this.)

'We pay for this tent and only we are allowed to pray for people here. Get off this property now.'

I am not telling a word of a lie. They came close to me as if to pick me up by force. The two kids ran away never to be seen for a long time after that. They wanted nothing to do with Christianity. I walked or ran to my car in shock. In total shock. My pursuers stayed so close to me you would have thought I had an army with me and could blow fire and destroy the tent at any minute. I shook as I drove off. They almost pushed my car away.

Please remember that at this point I was a fairly new Christian. God was growing me up in fast forward. Satan knew that God had big plans and that I was a willing vessel. I was a hundred per cent dedicated. Jesus was my bread and butter and my day and my night. In Him I moved and had my being. One lady at my Bible Study once said that she was so happy because Satan knew her name. I thought this a very silly thing to say and did not understand. She said it meant that God had great plans for her life.

I arrived home so shaken, I could hardly put my finger in the direction of my Bible Study leader's number on the dial. Bev and Ampie had a big job calming me down. Ampie asked me if I would be prepared to forgive these people as we might one day work together with the youth. Forgiveness was not on the list yet; I was trying to digest what had just happened. Surely this could not happen?

Jesus was, and is, and always will be faithful to me in my reading. My Lord had the answer right there where I was walking with Him in his Word at that time in my life.

Mark 3:22 says, 'But the teachers of religious law who had arrived from Jerusalem said, "He's possessed by Satan, the prince of demons. That's where He gets the power to cast out demons."'

Jesus was accused of being possessed by Satan and getting his power from Satan then why could the same thing not happen to me? He understood exactly how I was feeling and his comfort enfolded me.

> 'Instead, God chose things the world considers foolish in order to shame those who think they are wise. And He chose things that are powerless to shame those who are powerful. God chose things despised by the world, things counted as nothing at all, and used them to bring to nothing what the world considers important' (1 Cor 1:27, 29).

'Do you know who she is?'

The unsavoury person referred to above is me, as you might have guessed.

The following conversation happened behind the closed door of a church meeting. I was oblivious to it until very recently. Boy, this is just like a story from the Gospel.

The Sunday School superintendent was about to defend the redeemed ex-stripper of the 70s. He did not use the fact that I was running a full-blown youth group at my house, that his wife was my cell group leader and that he knew that I was sold out for Jesus. He did not use the fact that my gift was melting in with the love of Jesus for children. These facts were obviously not working in this scenario.

What he used was a handful of stones. Yes; a handful of stones which he pulled out of his pocket and laid on the table.

'Do you know who it is that you want to bring into the Sunday School as a teacher? Do you know who she is? You are not to touch her!' This was the minister of the church speaking.

The superintendent had his own question.

'Do you know who I am?'

'Yes, we do. You run the whole Sunday School. We know you.'

Superintendent: 'No, you don't know who I am. You know me from the church. You do not know who I was before Jesus redeemed me!'

It is at this point that the superintendent used the stones. (He must have known what the meeting was going to be about to have brought the stones along.) So just like Jesus, he asked the members of the church board to take one stone if they had no sins.

There are always two sides to a story. I could put on a mask and run and defend the minister on this side of the court and then put on the other mask and defend the redeemed stripper on the other side.

At the time that I was told about this incident, which happened more than 14 years ago, I was reading about Jesus being rejected at Nazareth. That had made me sad and I felt rejected by the people I need so much.

But now at the time of writing this I am reading through the book of Titus and God is showing me why I must forgive the rejection. In Titus 1 from verse 6 onwards it tells you what the behaviour of an 'elder' should be. Also in other parts of the Bible it is expected that people who serve in the church must live righteous lives.

The minister at that time did not know me, (unlike the ministers we have now). So it is understandable that he had to protect his church. I was known as a person with a public indecency conviction. When it comes to children it is better to be safe than sorry.

I thank the minister for having had the children's interest at heart and I thank the superintendent for taking the trouble to get to know me and to have heard God's voice saying that I was his chosen one, and if he used me, he was using Jesus.

Then my dear superintendent, this meeting must have made you nervous as I remember the classrooms being allocated to the teachers until at the end there was no classroom left and no children and one lone teacher still waiting patiently for a class. Two teenage boys came to the rescue as they were not ready to join the older kids in the teenage church. Of course that set off a new war with the teacher of the teenagers as I had 'stolen' two of her children. I had no idea what was going on. Oh, how I smile now when I see the devil at work.

> *The Bible says that the devil is like a roaring lion (1 Peter 5:8). He comes in the darkness, and tries to frighten the children of God with his mighty roar. But when you switch on the light of the Word of God, you discover that there is no lion. There is only a mouse with a microphone! Got it?*
> *REINHARD BONNKE*

What a wonderful lesson this was for me.

In Acts Chapter 9 God struck Paul blind and then God brought in a disciple to come and give him sight. Ananias is all, 'Here I am, Lord,' until he hears who he has to go and see. God allows him to bad-mouth Paul and explain why he should not go. What the Lord says to Ananias then made me sit up: 'Go, for he is a chosen vessel of Mine to bear My name before Gentiles, kings, and the children of Israel ....' It is never for us to decide who we will and will not pray for or teach. The rest of Paul's life is history. One of these two children could be a Paul of the future.

God's work is about individuals. Jesus died for me. Jesus died for you. Who was I to complain that I had only two children in my Sunday School class. These were the most important individuals to God. During that year God opened up his treasures for us in a wonderful way.

Then for the next couple of years I had big Sunday School classes and never stopped loving teaching and loving the children. I think after five years I stopped because Peter and I were preparing to leave to live in England for good.

This idea of going to England because my husband wanted to, annoyed my sister Linda beyond reason. She said that I was spineless and that I should say no.

I tried to explain to her that Jesus teaches us to obey our husbands. Our husbands can do nothing if God does not agree. If God does not want us to go to live in England, then we won't live in England. Everything is in God's hands and He wants obedience from us. We were in England for two or three months and then came back. It never did happen that we lived there permanently. It was on our return that I went to work at the Bluff Christian Academy.

My Alzheimer's mother

Judge not, that you be not judged.
– MATTHEW 7:1

Whatever part of my reputation had not been destroyed by my stripping, was destroyed by my mother. As I mentioned before, my mother had Alzheimer's Disease.

Due to her mental condition, she told people negative things about me and ran me down in such a way that it sounded really convincing. This had the effect that the people at my church believed her.

I reached breaking point when one of the ladies at church came up to me and accused me openly of abusing my mother. This was the last straw. I asked her to please take my mother and look after her for one day; just for one single day and then come back to me. She took her. I helped her put my mother into her car. They dropped her back at my house in the afternoon.

The next Sunday I was sitting in church when the lady concerned came down the aisle towards me. She knelt in front of me and begged for forgiveness. She said that she had had no idea of how bad my mother's medical condition was or of how difficult my mother could be. She apologized for having judged me.

She told me that she had taken my mother into her home for the day, pampered her with tea and cake and a deliciously prepared meal. This lady lived in a cottage on her daughter's property. Apparently, sometime after lunch my mother had run up to the main house and asked the lady's daughter to let her in. She asked the daughter to please give her something to eat and drink, even if it was a dry piece of bread. She said she had been visiting for a whole day with a woman in the cottage and had had nothing to eat or drink for all of that time.

This lady did not know that one of the effects of Alzheimer's disease is short-term memory loss, and that my mother could not remember having had tea and cake, or lunch.

The lady told me that she had been beside herself at my mother's apparent rudeness. She had called my mother a liar and an ungrateful woman and brought her back home to me.

Many other church members were unaware of the personality changes that Alzheimers sufferers undergo, or of the bizarre behaviour they display. They were also totally oblivious to the physical and emotional demands that caring for my mother made on me.

My mother would come to the Sunday School door when my kids were leaving to go home. She would approach the parents and ask if they had a room for her. She said I was a lovely daughter but she understood that I needed my space and wanted her out of the house.

The children's parents had believed my mother when she told them these things and that I did not care for her.

At my mother's funeral one of the leading church ladies (with whom I work and whom I love today), told me it was a shame that I cared for my mother only now at her funeral but that I had not cared about her when she was alive.

I gave my mother the freedom of my house and garden to do whatever she wanted to with her flowerpots and plants. I gave her the main bedroom and took the smallest room for myself. I was always struggling with God, who was teaching me to get my priorities right. My kingdom was in heaven. I had to show him that things don't matter.

Many a day I cried out to God: 'Lord you give me more than I can take!'

When I had reached breaking point and sent my mother to one of my sisters, my sister was unable to cope and began to show symptoms of a nervous breakdown after only three days.

She gave my mother sleeping pills and locked her in her room. Then she passed her on to the next sister. Joanie managed for over a year but by then her whole family was falling apart.

Just when caring for our mother was becoming impossible for all of us, God, in a miraculous way, opened a door for her at the Natal Settlers Home in Durban. So all five of us sisters met at my house with my mother and we took her to her new 'home'.

Left to right: Glenda, Mother, Hermie, Joan in front, Linda, and Jean (standing)

I kept a close watch on her well-being and brought her home to my house every weekend. Part of her illness was that she underwent a personality change. She hated me and believed I wanted to kill her. She would climb over the wall and run away into the street. Despite all this I cared for her lovingly. In Exodus 20:12 we are told, 'Honor your father and mother. Then you will live a long, full life in the land the Lord your God is giving you.'

I did my mother's washing and spring-cleaned her room on the weekends as I was teaching at the time. I groomed her hair and nails at home and loved her with all my heart. You see, I do things for Jesus and not for man.

I would go to the Home on weekdays at five o'clock in the morning, before going to work, and sit under the window where they were bathing my mother, to check up on the way they were talking to her and treating her.

I stayed with my church because they truly did not understand my situation. I had fallen into the same trap with one of my mother's friends. I thought his children had been cruel for taking the house away from under him and putting him in a place of care. I realized something was wrong after his third visit to our house when he spoke the identical words as the times before. I found out he was falling and leaving the stove on and getting into all sorts of trouble. People don't know these things and are quick to blame the children.

My sisters also apologized to me as they had believed everything my mother had said about Peter and me until they took her into their homes. At the funeral my sister Hermie tried to explain this to the congregation — about what I had been through. It just sounded like excuses and they were not convinced.

Four days before my mother died she was moved to frail care. It was a long weekend. I stayed by her side day and night. Linda came at night and we both slept in her room. I slept in the bed with her, holding her, and Linda slept on the chair.

On the second-last day I talked about Jesus. I sang songs. I saw my mother lift her arms in praise. I said the Sinner's Prayer to her and read about the room that Jesus went to prepare for her. (The Sinner's Prayer will be found in Appendix A.)

Then a strange thing happened; her mind became so clear. She asked to talk to my brother Dale and all my sisters. I phoned them and she had a normal conversation with them, remembering their children and circumstances. She spoke to Dale as if he was there with her. But the saddest part for me was … she never recognized me. She never said my name.

I went home to have one night's good sleep. She died that night.

I did not know she had died. I prepared for the next day's visit.

My name was on my mother's forms as the contact person but when my mother was dying they called Linda. However, Linda is not well and does not answer her phone at night. She only got the message the next day. Everyone knew our mother had died, but not me. I packed some yoghurt and nappies for my mother and went to visit. She was dead.

You must know that God, Jesus, the Holy Spirit and I had some very intense conversations. If the home had phoned me I would have rushed there and would have been able to say goodbye. God said He did not want me to do that. Everything was in his hands and He knows what is best for me. No one can do anything in my life that He does not okay. I must trust Him. He loves me. He has plans to use my experiences to bless others. God gave me the peace that passes all understanding. I was filled with a joy that is indescribable. For me to live is Christ.

'Judge not, that you be not judged …' (Matt 7:1, NKJV).

'Obviously, I'm not trying to win the approval of people, but of God. If pleasing people were my goal, I would not be Christ's servant' (Gal 1:10).

'Do you know who you have brought into our church?'

Oh no, not again! This time it was a church in Durban. The denomination was the one I grew up in and which I believed had changed.

Should I not feel like something the cat had dragged in?

Now you know why I am a Jesus fanatic. I have to be in the Word all the time to know who I am in Christ, so that when the devil attacks, I can tell him to get behind me, for I know in whom I believe.

In Acts 2:44 it says, 'And all the believers met together in one place and shared everything they had.' I am all for this, especially to get to the results at the end of the chapter, which says, 'And each day the Lord added to their fellowship those who were being saved.'

So when Amanda, a member of this church I am speaking about, asked to borrow my puppets for the church to use, I opened the door and said, 'Take them all. Use them for the glory of God. I will ask for them back if I need them.' Some months later she returned them.

Sometime after that, I got a call from a desperate Amanda. She had to do a puppet show the next day at her church and she had forgotten about it. She was writing exams and had no time. Please would I do a puppet show for her?

What a pleasure. No greater joy than to bring God's Word to the children.

My faithful friend Eliza was there before I could finish my request and we got ready to do the *Redemption Story* puppet play on the Sunday morning.

The next day, the deacon walked over to us where we were setting up our puppets. He did not look at Eliza or me, but straight at Amanda. 'Do you know who you have brought into our church!? Did you tell the minister?'

That bad taste in my heart feeling came up.

Amanda did not know who I was. The deacon did, and the minister knew as well, as I had invited him to our concert not long before. No turning back now. God does as God does.

I thank God for children. They look straight into your heart and take readily from what God has to offer from there.

We had no welcome, no greeting and no goodbye. I stood before those people as if Jesus had no power in my life. Jesus can do only so much, but when it comes to a stripper these people knew much more than God. God had his limits, as far as they were concerned. But not the children.

Restrictions were put on me from the start. They gave me a mike I had to hold while talking into it so I had no hands to manoeuvre the puppets.

Eliza was so good, doing the things I normally do. At one stage she tried to hold the mike for me and our arms got all tangled up. She was too short to hold the 'God light' at the top of the wooden cross where it was fixed to the puppet box. I could not talk and move with the mike. Eliza was on her toes stretching out to help me, but to no avail. Actually, looking back, it was very funny. The things God does with us two old ladies! The end result was amazing. The children took two rulers from me and formed them into a cross to explain exactly what Christianity is and how Jesus had died for us to bring us back into the presence of God.

That was what it was about. The children's hearts were not hardened. They knew that by inviting Jesus into their hearts they are reborn.

It was God's plan from the beginning of creation that Eliza and I would be there at that moment in that church and with those children. We were obedient and God's Word would do what it was sent out to do. Nothing can come between us and the love of God.

Sometimes I wonder why God chooses me to do a job that could be done by so many people with good reputations. But all the time I thank God that He can use me with, and in spite of, and because of my bad reputation. I thank God that He does not look at us as Man does. He looks at the heart.

'... If they are planning and doing these things merely on their own, it will soon be overthrown. But if it is from God, you will not be able to overthrow them. You may even find yourselves fighting against God!' (Acts 5:38–39).

'Don't let anyone capture you with empty philosophies and high sounding nonsense that come from human thinking and from the spiritual powers of this world, rather than from Christ' (Col 2:8).

Another time

You know there are times when I get tired of trying to find a reason for people's rude behaviour. This next episode could be the way in which this person mourned, but as for me, as I feel at this moment, I wipe the dust off my feet and move on.

In April 2011 I was at a deathbed where the doctor was waiting for a life-or-death decision and the family was at loggerheads and accusations were flying in all directions. I intervened and asked if we could pray and bring our Lord into our emotions and decisions and to fill us with His love. I touched the one person and said: 'Let us hold hands and pray about this.' I felt the Pharisee turn into a pillar of salt. It is easy to read people's thoughts as Jesus did. I could put these words above her head with bubbles as they do in the cartoons: 'Pray with you?!! You stripper!'

The actual words she used were (as she pulled her shoulder away from my touch and cast her face into granite): 'No! I have already prayed. And whether you like it or not, I have told God what to do!'

So these are the things that humans are made of. Whichever side we are on, we sure need the love of God to set us free. I wondered if I would have been prepared to sit with Hitler and pray in love for him? I apologized to God and tried to see the fingers that point at me too.

God, why is it so hard for people to believe that I am truly your child? Why does it hurt me? Why does it bother me today?

'Why are you not helping in the kitchen?'

Don't expect the smell of homemade anything, should you ever come to visit me. Shop biscuits and juice are the norm. I don't even have two matching glasses. I am generally known as undomesticated.

My favourite food is peanut butter and I eat anything anyone else makes. Peter, my husband does all the cooking and loves it.

I am a good example of the body of Christ consisting of different parts. If the chef is the neck, then I am the toenail; far removed from the neck.

'Why are you not helping in the kitchen, if this is your church?' This is what I was asked by an acquaintance on visiting our church's food fête. I always have all the right and wisest answers to give to anyone once they have walked away and left me standing stupid: 'Hello, I have ten thumbs. Thank me for not being in the kitchen.'

For many years I served on a team making and delivering sandwiches for the schools. I would make two for every six Eliza made.

The gifts I do have, God draws out of me without leaving a stone unturned. Not always visible to the eye. God knows.

I once told the kids in the youth group about a good deed I had done. I said that we should not normally talk about such deeds as they are between ourselves and God. But I wanted them to realize that the church is not a building — we as individuals are the church — and that what you give to others you are giving to God. I told them that a stranger once came into the church for prayer. She was cold and needed a blanket. The church had nothing on hand. Not true; I am the church and I have a blanket. So I took the woman to my house. She waited in the car while I fetched a Bible and a blanket and food. I stood there juggling my thoughts. My hand on the old duvet, my hand on my brand new duvet: 'Eeny, meeny, miny, mo.' What we give to others we are giving to God .... God forbid I give Him an old duvet the dog had slept on. I took my new duvet and gave it to the woman. I am telling you about this for the same reason that I told the youth about it. Some things are between God and us only, and so it should be. So if you think someone is lazy, tell God, not them. He knows.

I should sign this 'Mary', and thank God for my 'Martha' friends.

I had sold my house in Johannesburg and converted the Durban house into self-contained single rooms. Not a single tenant passes through my gates without the love of Jesus filling my heart for them and praying for their names to be put into the Book of Life.

Kimmie went to London on 7 March 2002.

My heart broke.

My mother had gone to live with Joan to give me a break after 18 years. Later she was accepted as a resident in the Natal Settlers Home near me.

I looked after my stepdaughter's baby boy for six months. When Peter's daughter brought Jethro to us from England during 2002 he was a bonny six-month-old baby.

In January 2003 we left for London, taking Jethro with us, to return him to his mother. By then he was a one-year-old little boy who could walk to his mommy.

We planned to live in London forever — our plans. We threw the dice but God's number was not the one we called.

We had sold almost everything in South Africa. The idea was that I would go back to South Africa three months after our returning the baby and getting settled in England. I would then sell the Durban house or rent it out to permanent tenants and do the other final things as Peter was already established in a job in London.

Nanny

While I was in England I advertised my services as a 'granny nanny' and experienced what it was like being a cleaning lady and caring for children. Life with Jesus is one big adventure.

Eduardo was the first child I cared for. An angry little man. But with all the surprises I had in my pockets and the love in my heart he was melted before I even carried him up the stairs to the playroom.

One weekend when his parents were away and I was in charge of him, he was very sick. I pulled my bed next to his and sponged him off with cool water to keep his temperature down. I prayed for him. The next day he was better. Every day before I left I would put love letters from Jesus under his and his brother's pillows. We put blankets over the desks, sat underneath and told stories by torchlight. We visited the library. I told Eduardo all about Jesus. His brother listened too and was surprised to know that the Bible was not just a storybook. Eduardo told all his friends that his nanny prayed for him and that Jesus healed him.

'O Lord, bless Eduardo abundantly.'

In the other nanny job I had, I resigned just as my employer fired me.

I was nanny number … 6 or 7 or 8 in a period of 8 weeks.

Scene one:

Josh, the four-year-old, wants milk on his cereal. I put a bit more milk onto his cereal. Josh wants more milk. I put a little more. Josh wants more. I put another drop. Josh screams: 'You put too much milk.' Josh turns the cereal bowl upside down on the table. The mother tells me to pick it up and give the child more cereal.

Scene two:

Play room. Play room? Toys and toys and toys. Shelves of toys from floor to ceiling. Children enter: throw toys off shelves. Puzzles after puzzles thrown out of boxes. Assembled toys dissembled and thrown around. Lots of empty shelves. Lots of toys covered the floor.

Mother: 'Take the kids for a walk and put away the toys!'

Put away the toys?

Kids scream!

The four-year-old had a big poo in his pants.

I put the toys in the shelves; just any old shelf. Big mistake. (If you had left me there for the rest of the year I still would not have known which shelf each toy lived on.)

Take screaming boy to the bathroom. Clean him. Wash his soiled clothes. Bath and dress him.

Enter mother: 'You did not put the toys away in the right places.'

Me: 'I had to come and clean Josh.'

Scene three:

Mother: 'When you have cooked, wash the floor.'

I finish the food and start mopping the floor.

Mother: 'Josh is tired, put him to bed right now.'

I leave the mop and water and carry the screaming child upstairs. I put him in his bed. He is still screaming his head off.

I prayed softly in my mind:

'Oh, Jesus, fill Josh with your peace and give him sleep.'

Josh screams even louder. 'Please, Jesus, You can do it.' Josh screams even louder. I stare into an unanswered prayer and wonder where Jesus is. Mother storms in ….

Mother: 'What are you doing? You left the mop in the water and the floor half washed.'

Me: 'You said I must take Josh up immediately.'

'Oh, Jesus, why are you letting this happen?'

That is how it happened that I resigned and she fired me at the same time. A very humbling experience and one that took me back to think of households in South Africa where many nannies were treated like this. I have a stone in the bottom of my wardrobe with the name of those two children written on it — Josh and Gracie. Both Bible names. My prayers for them are safely received in the Kingdom and God has put his stamp on them.

'May this family be blessed in abundance. May God be glorified in the lives of Josh and Gracie. All Glory to Jesus.'

Then there was Al, short for Alexander. Al was bright and beautiful. I believe we both made an eternal impression on each other. One day Al will tell the story of the stories I told him and the time we had together. His father was German and his mother Japanese. They tried to contact me years later to come back to look after their young man, but I was back in South Africa teaching at a Christian school.

My diaries recall afresh all these experiences and the verses that covered every aspect of my days there.

Moving to England did not happen.

16

Teaching at Bluff Christian Academy (2003-2006)

The start of my interview with the Headmistress of the school was no different from any normal interview for a post. We smiled a lot and talked of our love for Jesus and for children. I knew the teaching position was as good as mine.

'There is one thing I must tell you, though,' I said. 'I was Glenda Kemp the stripper.'

Silence. I thought she had stopped breathing. Her face was going red.

'But Jesus has cleansed me! I am a new person in Christ.'

She asked me to leave her office so that she could compose herself.

'I will call you; don't call me,' were her final words.

My tears were already flowing before I could get into the privacy of my home to unpack it all before God.

'But Lord, the same Spirit that is in me is in her, then why, Lord, does she reject me for my past which does not even exist anymore because you took it away?'

The next day I got a call from the Headmistress to come and see her. The living God we serve had spoken to her through a message that was sent to her husband that day. It was a story about a minister who married a woman with a 'past'. The congregation would not accept her. In so doing they were rejecting Jesus. They were saying that his death on the cross was not powerful enough to remove all sins. The blood was on their hands. The job was mine.

This system was amazing. This school is amazing. I was able to talk about what was in my heart and soul and mind — Jesus. The children work in offices from books that are self-explanatory.

I started off helping out with Grade 12, then moved to Grades 5, 6 and 7 (in one class) and ended up teaching Grade 1 for two years. There are many eternal treasures that I built up in heaven in the four years that I taught at this school. Jesus made provision for my weakness by providing wonderful mothers to assist me in organizing the red tape for me. The love of the Lord for the children was stuck onto me like glitter on glue. The preciousness of those children to God made the school holy ground to be stepped on with love and care at all times.

All I had, and more, I put in. That is what God asks of us. If I fail it is never because I did not give my all; it is that my all is not enough. God called me to be faithful, and that I was.

The most important part of my life was the early morning hours spent with Jesus in the Word. No matter how tired, my alarm was set for four o'clock in the morning to speak to my Father and to hear his voice.

For the hot summer months I froze water which I kept in my classroom for any child to come and drink. I made sure they knew that Jesus was the one who provided water to quench our thirst. My clown puppet named 'Savie' had a story to tell. He wanted everyone to know he was saved. His red nose reminded him of the blood of Jesus who died for him. The white paint on his face was to show how white his life becomes when Jesus removes the sin. He is a clown because Jesus wants us to be joyful. Savie would dance to music if anyone could memorize a Bible verse. It was amazing how children from pre-school to Grade 12 would line up to recite Bible verses so they could see me manipulate Savie into a dance. I also had other puppets with Jesus messages.

The opportunity to witness was never-ending. I often gave up my break to explain about Jesus or listen to problems. Every Grade 1 child knew that the reason they were learning to read was so that they could read the Word of God for themselves and so that no one would be able to lead them astray.

They would know the truth. Because it was a Christian school, Jesus was King and God was glorified.

Visiting London again

I spent three weeks with my darling daughter in the July 2006 school holidays.

Going back to places, now in the presence of Jesus, was a totally new experience. I walked Brewer Street; looked at pictures of naked ladies at Paul Raymond's Revue Bar; and stood at the back stage door rejoicing at my new life. I had a life now. One that would continue into eternity. I prayed for the working ladies who danced on the stage on which I had danced. May they have a life too, one that would last forever, in Jesus.

My diaries tell how I spent my holiday in London. Reading and rereading the wonderful Word of God while my child was at work. Then Kimmie and me just being together and talking. Blessing after blessing after blessing.

And then back to work.

The last straw that broke the camel's back

I was given break duty every day at school. Teaching Grade 1 children made this hard as they always needed help in some or other area, which normally took half my break.

I complained to God. I always take my complaints to Him before going anywhere else. He showed me that I was working for Him and for no one else and I must walk the extra mile. I was feeling my age and becoming very tired and forgetful. I knew later that God was using these signs to finish my season at the school. I handed in my notice but stayed until the end of the year. My prayers and my love for those children will follow me into heaven. God will bless them more than I can ever ask for or imagine.

Retirement (ha ha) — 2007

You won't find the word 'retirement' in the Bible.

It was a great feeling when school started again in January 2007 and I could drive to the beach with my dog. Spare time in Bible language means intensive personal time with God. Time without God is trash and not worth having.

Glenda and Eliza with Savie the puppet

Before you could say 'time' I was already involved with my next door neighbour, delivering food to the needy and renting out her rooms which she had converted to self-contained rooms like mine. More people to pray for. God never sends you the wrong tenants. The wrong tenants are the right ones for Him.

Eliza and I were spending every cent we had on buying Bibles. We handed them out wherever we found ourselves. Every Bible was handed out with an instruction sheet on *Steps to Peace with God* which I found in The *Billy Graham Christian Worker's Handbook*. On the other side of the pamphlet I reprinted (with the permission of *Joy* magazine), *Biblically-based answers by Val Waldeck*. Everything I did was taken to my minister for approval and done under the auspices of my church.

A description follows of a typical day in our lives as Eliza and I act as God's postmen.

I am a postman — your heart is a postbox

At the ripe old age of 63 I am experiencing the adventures of a postman's life as if I am recreating *Treasure Island*, map and all. 'You are here!' is the circle drawn around my house on the black and white copy of my area map. The other circle is round my friend Eliza's house. Where we differ from *Treasure Island* is that we already have the treasure and the burial spots are everywhere our feet (or in my case, my knees), can carry us. We start off at 'Jerusalem'; that is where we live, my friend and I. Then the bright yellow highlighter spreads along the roads on the map in hot pursuit of our 'beautiful' wrinkled feet.

We are *Candid Camera* material, the two of us. I am not fat but next to Eliza anyone is fat. I am not unfit, but next to Eliza anyone is unfit. I am not slow.... OK, I am slow but next to Eliza anyone is slow. Eliza shoots forward down the road like a conveyer belt delivering its merchandise precisely on schedule. I am the juggling clown at the back. With a bit of a sprint from my side and a bit of a crossover delivery on her side, the two of us are side by side, playing *Postman Pat* on our respective sides of the road.

Eliza is in the street to bring the reading to the people. I am in the street to read to the people as I 'open' their houses like rows of books in a library, with titles as varied as fingerprints. Decorated with their own dogs, gardens, alterations and, of course, their very personal postboxes. By the time I get home I pocket the same thrills and excitement as I would have gained from a holiday to Las Vegas or a trip to Disneyland or a dream island; whichever you choose.

Postbox hearts

Go and take a look at your postbox and see your heart.

Mine? A bit dilapidated. A fair share of glue and repair visible. Mine could do with some TLC. The saw fixed the dilemma of branches bullying the postman into physical exercise getting the incoming mail into the 'inbox'. Keep an eye on the overgrowth. One house put unfriendly mesh wire directly in front of the opening, making the mail delivery a challenge if not a complete failure. I guess we have to guard our hearts.

Some people don't have a postbox. Anyone can read the invisible sign: 'Stay out!' There is always a way in, over the wall. It reminds me of the parable of the sower who planted the seed. The mail drops wherever it drops and no one knows if the thorns got it or the fertile ground. But I do know it was dropped.

If ladders were not so heavy to carry around, a postman would do well to invest in one. Those 'sky-scraper' postboxes that first make you practise your monkey-glide as you go down the dip and then laugh at you when it tells you that you fall short of its high standard. Who needs a gym? After these stretch exercises you get the 'bend-down-low' postboxes that remind you of the instruction to be humble and send you on your way with a hop, a skip and a jump.

Then there is the 'total wipeout' postbox. The trick is to get your hand holding the mail to the right spot at the right time without having the jumping dogs snatch your hand into their snapping jaws. Postmen should not only get danger money but 'dog entertainment' money as well. Touch a postbox and your fate is sealed and delivered by the canine species as guilty as 'charged'. Advertisement for postmen: 'Only tall, inventive, former athletes will be considered for these vacancies.'

'For the spirit is willing, but the body is weak!' (Matt 26:41). Now this point is only reached when the 200-odd pamphlets for the day have been delivered into the postboxes, and the way home is long and we are empty-handed. Only then do we call on Robbie, the wheels belonging to our 911 number. He finds us panting somewhere on the corner of anywhere and nowhere and safely delivers us back home. Mission accomplished until further notice from my knees, Eliza's back and Bluff Printers.

Just what is this 'thing' we deliver so fervently? ...

(See Appendix A for details of these pamphlets.)

* * * * *

The bushes at the beach were giving me a lot of instructions from God.

By the time the next God-given task came along, my neighbour had moved into another mode and the short season ended.

17

From my diary

14 November 2008 — lost my dog!

My testimony follows, as read out one Sunday in church …

'Lost my dog. Yet I will rejoice in the Lord.

'The emphasis of what I have to share today is not on the miraculous outcome, but on the way the Word of God sustained me when it seemed like the bottom had fallen out of my world on Friday afternoon. I had prepared to share the greatness of our God whatever the outcome would be.

'If you know me, or are a dog person, you will understand what I experienced when my dog, Jedi, went missing from my car in the thunderstorm we had on Friday afternoon; and the emotions as my friends and I searched the area until the sun went down. During this search, near Grosvenor Girls' High School, a couple who happened to walk out of their house to their garage, and who happened to be from our church, took my number and helped in the search. They were Colleen and Fred.

'I always carry messages from the Word in my pocket to hand out to whoever is in need of them. Here I was, desperately in need of my Lord's audible Word. I pulled out the Word, like a pill to put under my tongue in the case of a threatened heart attack.

'Do not be afraid, for I have ransomed you. I have called you by name; you are mine. When you go through deep waters, I will be with you. When you go through river of difficulty, you will not drown. When you walk through the fire of oppression, you will not be burned up; the flames will not consume you' (Isaiah 43:1–2).

'I prayed:

'Oh, Jesus, am I glad I belong to you. Am I glad you are not a "break the glass in case of emergency" God to me. Jesus, you know how much I love my dog, but if I never find her again I will praise you. You lent her to me and I have been a good steward Lord. Thank you for the joy you gave me through my dog.'

Driving Miss Jedi

'I remembered Habakkuk 3:17–19 which says: "Even though the fig trees have no blossoms, and there are no grapes on the vines; even though the olive crop fails, and the fields lie empty and barren; even though the flocks die in the fields, and the cattle barns are empty, Yet I will rejoice in the LORD! I will be joyful in the God of my salvation! The Sovereign Lord is my strength! He makes me as surefooted as a deer, able to tread upon the heights."

'Getting home, I ran to my diary to see what my reading had been that morning. Do you know that in all my 14 years of being in a relationship with

Jesus, I have never had a reading that was not relevant for that day on which it was given to me. It was from Daniel 3:4 onwards. (I was following the readings at the back of *Faith for Daily Living*. But I had skipped that week's reading because I did not feel for reading about end times, but I loved the next week's topic which was on music, so I read that.) It was about having to bow down before Nebuchadnezzar's gold statue when the music played. I refuse to bow down to the bad music, to the gold statue. I was bought with the blood of Christ and not with silver or gold. I look at that which cannot be seen. That which is forever. The evil one touches me not. I made a decision: Every time the longing and pain for my dog came, I would praise God, I would pray for a lost soul. I prayed throughout the night. I pleaded. For every one of my neighbours on each side, for my family, for my tenants, for the bush people. I prayed from my heart and soul and mind.

'I know that all that matters is that our names are written in the Book of Life. To seek first the Kingdom of God. Do you know the comfort when God said to me "Fear not, for I have redeemed you. I have called you by name." (What matters is not that my dog is found or not found but that my name is written in the Book of Life.) Has God redeemed you? Is your name written in the Book of Life? Are you not sure? Make sure today. If you want to make Jesus Christ your Lord and your Saviour then you can come forward at the end of the service and we will pray with you.

'Oh yes, I almost forgot. Colleen and Fred phoned me at 5:30 a.m. on Saturday morning. My dog was found curled up in a corner of the wall by their garage. All praise be to God forever and ever. Amen.'

Music and Jesus and me

My excitement alarm went off when I read in Revelation 15:3 that the song of Moses was sung in heaven. Moses sang the song here on earth and now there it was in heaven.

Before I could reach the record player as a child, my heart began to beat to the rhythm of music. I did not need the gift of a voice or the ability to play a musical instrument because God gave me the gift of voices and instruments putting things into me. For years I danced my gifts on the wrong plains. Then God put my feet on his soil and musical ears unwrapped ladders that helped

147

me climb to places where I could socialize and party with Jesus in indescribable joy.

I dare you, wake me up in the middle of the night and see if the CD player in my head is disconnected? There is a never-ending source of energy finding the back of the net to score a praise goal to God. Music is like speaking in tongues as it brings out languages that you cannot otherwise utter.

When God gives us a gift it is to be used to serve others. So when God is glorified in a song and melody by a gifted singer or writer, it finds its way down the years to overwhelm and bless someone like me. What an impacting thought. God has you and me in mind when he gives to others.

Sometimes a song stops and I have more to say. Then God provides the words to the existing melody. This was the case when in my quiet time I was singing the following words to the tune of the well-known hymn *How Great Thou Art*.

> 'And Lord Your Word, while reading true and humbly
>
> Unlocks a world and finds you face to face.
>
> Wordless I fall before your Godly greatness
>
> And Lord, proclaim how great your word explains.
>
> Then sings my soul, my saviour God, to Thee,
>
> "How great Thou art, how great Thou art."'

Then the song continues when I get to the beach:

> 'When by the sea, I see the waves performing
>
> Lifting foam hands that shout with joy and glee
>
> The sounds and moves, bursting with all its praising
>
> Pointing to God, the God that we must please.
>
> Then sings my soul, my Saviour God, to Thee.
>
> "How great though art, how great Thou art."'

Then there is the annoying time when a worldly song will find its way in and has no way out. It gets trapped in my head making a lovely noise with no words to remind me of the One I am walking with.

Please don't get me wrong, there is nothing wrong with enjoying songs that do not sing God's message or praises. It is just something personal to me. It is a constant desire in my soul that longs to bring God into all I do and see and hear.

When we sisters get together, it is the music that brings us into a song and dance and lots of laughter. The older we get, the more laughter. Being Afrikaner ladies, it is the Afrikaner songs that bring the youth back into our bones.

Who needs a singing voice and musical gifts to praise God? Even the stones can praise God, so I will most certainly do it with everything at my disposal. The world is the Lord's and the fullness thereof; I will praise Him with it.

Working with children and becoming like children just brings forth an endless opportunity to sing and dance his praises.

When working on a dance for the youth I often get Eliza, my soulmate, to come over to memorize it with me as I don't know how to choreograph dance movements. Here is an extract from my diary after one such session:

> 'It must be so funny seeing Eliza and me dancing here in the lounge. Two old bags dancing to "Celebrate Jesus, Celebrate", swinging our arms and jumping up and down and clapping hands. Surely God and the angels are looking and having a good laugh! Tomorrow her back and my knees will need a Disprin.'

Prayers and progress for Kim

My diaries speak of continuous struggles in prayer for Kimmie, who had set her heart on becoming a Speech Therapist. Her work with autistic children had brought her to the realization of where she wanted to be professionally. After completing a supplementary study year she was accepted at the University College of London (UCL). I had spent the day of her interview on my knees before my Father, pleading for my child; just as Jesus pleads for me. I spend a lot of time on my knees seeking to know God more and more. I never cease to stand in amazement at the revelation of his Word.

Glenda Kemp - Snake Dancer

18

Bluff Methodist Church Youth Group

In 2008 two new ministers were appointed to serve at our Bluff Methodist Church — Rev. Hugh Jenkins and Rev. Joani Geldenhuys-Jenkins — two fully-pledged ministers who happened to be married and who had two beautiful teenage children. This family not only entered our church but into the lives of its members; most certainly mine.

My love of evangelizing wherever I walked and of expressing the joy of the Lord that rises above (or because of) obstacles, came to Hugh's attention. When he learnt about my puppets he asked if I would start a youth group open to children in Grades 4 to 7. After much prayer I said 'Yes' to Jesus. I say 'much prayer' because I know that when the Lord takes me on a journey it is the full journey and the joy of the Lord will literally be all the strength that I need.

I looked forward to sharing with the children the wonderful Word of Jesus that provides a weekly testimony of a living Christ. Eliza was right there by my side encouraging and overflowing with Jesus' love to all who came close to her. Pam Classen was the games lady and organizer. Hugh and Joani's teenage daughter, Stephany Jenkins, was the all-round helper. Youth and age balanced the scales. It was through Pam's thinking that Jesus gave us the name for the group — 'J-Zone' — (Jesus-Zone). We were now stepping into Jesus' territory — most sacred ground where the youth is touched.

J-Zone — 2009

I have a photo of every child who stops over or who finds rest at J-Zone. My face lights up at the sight of each child whom God has allowed to be where his light shines. No visit is a coincidence. Knowing Jesus and knowing that our lives were planned before the beginning of creation makes us stand in wonder of the love and mercy of the God who created the universe and everything in it.

Through the focus on J-Zone many 'God treasures' began to flow out of my resources. In order to bring the Word of God to the children's full understanding I made use of actions, plays, art, dance and songs.

Every J-Zone creation came to me from Jesus in the small hours of the night. With the faces of these precious individuals my time, energy and money went where my heart is.

'Jesus replied: "Your mistake is that you don't know the Scriptures, and you don't know the power of God"' (Matt 22:29).

My first instruction! Read and pray.

The children had no idea that the Bible was written for them. I started by typing out the book of Mark and showing them how to talk to Jesus in response to what He was saying to them.

2009 Concert — 'Go tell it on the mountain!'

I decided that if something was going to be done regarding a theatrical production, the best time to do it would be right away. So I took all the plays, songs and dances we had been doing over the previous six months and staged a play with the children. It was hard work and not without opposition from within. It was a wonderful experience that would leave a Jesus mark on every child and prayerfully, on those who attended it.

It is so good to remember the blessings but to get to the blessings there is often a barrage of enemy attacks to get through. The first of these concerned a member of my family.

Family tragedy

My sister Jean died. At her funeral in Johannesburg I experienced inconsolable sorrow. I flew back just in time for the concert. When I say that God carries his children, I know what I am talking about.

The next attack occurred on the morning of the concert.

The enemy attacks the concert preparations!

The night before the concert, which was to be on a Sunday morning, Eliza and I had worked until late to get everything ready. Nothing was too much trouble for us. We stuck chocolate coins under each of the 100 chairs and then painstakingly and prayerfully went through the checklist putting everything in place ready for the concert.

The next morning everything looked just as we had left it the night before.

The curtains opened: Showtime!

The children were in high spirits. And the Spirit was high.

The second item was a play and it went smoothly. The angels appeared at the set time. I was the narrator, and from where I was positioned in front, I thought they looked a bit different but they were beautiful. What I did not know is that Eliza was handling a crisis backstage and she believes that only a miracle had got the angels on stage in time. Someone had pulled all the ribbons out of the angels' dresses. The ribbons were what held the dresses up. Eliza prayed as the Holy Spirit moved her hands to tie knots to keep the dresses where they should be.

The next crisis was with the clown item. Verses that were pinned onto the clown suit had been ripped off and the props he had to use were missing! We improvised.

The last item in the concert involved all the children. Here too, parts of the children's costumes had been mixed up and others were missing. The curtain was ready to open. The child playing the leading role did not have the pom-pom she needed as a prop. She sat down flat, folded her arms and refused to act. That was when the devil finally managed to rob me of my joy and I shouted at her in a very unchristian manner. My dear friend Eliza came to the rescue by providing a pom-pom to save the situation. Stephanie, our compère, was covering up the delay by telling jokes and stories from resources she did not know she had. When the curtain finally opened nobody in the audience was aware there had been any mishap.

Up to this day we do not know who had tried to disrupt our performance. We found all of the missing things, though. Someone had pulled the ribbons out of the angels' costumes, removed the pom-poms and just thrown everything to the very back of the stage.

J-Zone concert

If the enemy gets so upset about God's plans then I know that the victory is eternal.

The highlight of the concert was the clown act. In this short play, Savie, the clown with the red nose, introduces the Lamb of God who died for the sins of the world. There was a new aspect to the act. One of my children, also dressed as a clown, sat on the chair next to Savie. Two silent puppets. Eliza and I interacted with the puppets. I spilt water and the big child 'puppet' comes to life and wipes it up. I am puzzled by the disappearance of the water. The children in the audience tell me it is the puppet but of course how can a puppet get up and do things? The lesson behind the act all boils down to us doing our good deeds in private.

There are many more plays and drama items that I am willing to share with you if you would like to present them in your youth groups. All you have to do is to write to me via the publisher's details on the Copyright page of this book.

19

More from my diary

December births of the past and the present

Deccember writings seem to bulge up and flow over in my diaries so why not share some with you?

When God chose 7 December for my little girl to be born, did He know that this little girl would later be the teenager who would focus my spiritual eyes back onto the birth of our Lord Jesus Christ? The birth that would take place inside of me and never stop growing again.

December 2009

Letter to my daughter on her birthday.

> 'Yesterday's memories walking through the Christmas spirit at the shops.
>
> Twenty-seven years ago this time, I was pregnant. Twenty-seven years ago this time Eliza had a little four-day-old girl. And 2000 years ago God was 21 days away from giving 'birth' to Jesus.
>
> The entire shopping centre was filled with pregnancy. The Spirit of the living God is being breathed by those who believe and those who don't believe. I marvel in my God who controls the universe and the

whole population that speaks the word "Christmas". The power of birth!

And you, Kimmie? Your delicate inner parts were already knit together in my womb. God's marvellous workmanship was lying inside my body. God was looking at you! He could have chosen any moment then to bring you into the open but he chose 7 December. His timing is always perfect. Every day of your life was recorded in His book. Every moment was laid out before a single day had passed. How precious are His thoughts about you? 13 Days before Christmas God took the wrapping off my present, and my eyes, for the first time, saw love. Thank You Father God, for this gift you gave me.

7 December 2009'

Even before she could read, Kim had riddles and rhymes and pictures to direct her to her birthday treasures that were hidden away. Now we have Jesus and the treasures he provides are beyond description.

'Happy birthday Kimmie

This morning I went to here: "Open for me the gates where the righteous enter and I will go in and thank the Lord. These gates lead to the presence of the Lord, and the godly enter there. I thank You for answering my prayers and giving me victory!" (Psalm 118:19–21). And while I was there God told me He is now your party organizer. He is the one rejoicing over you with a joyful song (Zephaniah 3:17) and wearing you like a signet ring on His finger (Haggai 2:23). Let the fun begin. Seek and you will find! The first present He gave you is also the clue to where all the other presents are hidden. The Bible! In Psalm 19:7 it gives you a layout of all that is hidden if you follow these instructions. These gifts are "more desirable than gold, even the finest gold. They are sweeter than honey, even honey dripping from the comb". What a gift!

Every year I relive your birth, from the moment of the first contraction to the bringing you home. I won't repeat it to you this year but I carry it in my heart. I could burst with happy emotion and it is as if your birth is like no other human being's birth. As if God did something for you and me that he never has and never will do for anyone else. Like it is our little secret. Why not? We all have our very own relationship with Him just as we have our own fingerprints, so why not our very own miraculous births.'

Blessings

Wikus — The cross, the man and the conviction

If you won the Lotto, who would you share it with? If you discovered eternal, abundant life, who would you share it with?

Wikus and the cross

It is only natural that the first people you would want to reel in would be your family.

When almost everyone in your family thinks you have seriously lost the plot and need to have your head examined, what do you do? When you become the family joker and are asked if you are rewriting the Bible, what do you do? You pray harder and love harder, that is what you do.

So what did I do when I got a call from my eldest sister Linda's son, asking if he and I could get together to pray earnestly for all of our family members?

I did a spiritual somersault and a spiritual 'thank and praise' fire display! Then, in preparation for our meeting I made a list of the names of all of my mother's children, grandchildren and great-grandchildren and spread it out on the table. Eliza had received instructions to be on her knees at her home to prepare the way for God's blessings to flow, and not to be interrupted by the evil one.

At 9 o'clock I looked out of the window. What I saw at the gate made my mouth hang open.

There at the gate was a big cross. The man bending under the weight of the cross was wet with perspiration.

The only man I know of with a cross, carried it 2000 years ago and his Name is Jesus. The Holy Spirit fills me to overflow with his Spirit.

'Oh, Wikus, how you must love Jesus! Oh, Jesus, how you must love Wikus!'

It was this love that made nothing of the 30 kilometres of ups and downs and witnessing to passers-by that lay between my house and Wikus' house. In my mind's eye I see Wikus carrying his heavy cross through the gates of eternity, and as he enters, the cross changes into a crown. The scene was set for an amazing altar offering for the souls of our loved ones.

The party began. Every seed from the Kemp family was handed over to eternity in God's open hand there in my lounge. We witnessed and encouraged each other, we read the Bible and shared experiences; we prayed, we praised, we made music and had Holy Communion. All this while standing in the gap for the family.

'We are human, but we don't wage war as humans do. We use God's mighty weapons, not worldly weapons, to knock down the strongholds of human reasoning and to destroy false arguments. We destroy every obstacle that keeps people from knowing God. We capture their rebellious thoughts and teach them to obey Christ.'

2 Corinthians 10:3–5

'My heart is filled with bitter sorrow and unending grief for my people, my Jewish brothers and sisters. I would be willing to be forever cursed – cut off from Christ! – if that would save them.'

Romans 9:2,3

'You will call and I will answer.'

Job 14:15

20

An eventful year

Yet what we suffer now is nothing compared to the glory He
will reveal to us later.

– ROMANS 8: 18

Before Easter of the year 2010 the 'black box' from the wreckage that crashed down on my life was found; but its secrets belong to God. Everything that had to do with penetrating my heart was recorded. Mark, a youth from my 1996 youth group, was dying of a heroin overdose. My sister Hermie lost both her daughter and her grandchild in a motor car accident. I was summoned to rush to my sister Joan's deathbed as she was dying from meningitis and had also had two strokes. And in the midst of all this, a film company was negotiating to make a movie of my life story and to distribute it internationally. South Africa was counting down the days to the 2012 FIFA World Cup soccer tournament and Kim and I were counting the days till her homecoming holiday.

A strange thing happened to me with the death of my sister Jean six months before the start of 2010. And now I was to have the same experience just before the death of Mark.

To understand what happened it is necessary for you to know that God is Spirit and God is not bound by time and space.

'But you must not forget this one thing, dear friends: A day is like a thousand years to the Lord, and a thousand years is like a day' (2 Pet 3:8).

Jean's death (not Joan)

Two telephones — the one being desperately clutched by Jean's friend Chammy, and the other by me — brought me to a closed door, behind which Jean was dying. Me in Durban; Chammy in a Johannesburg hospital.

They would not let Chammy into the room to put the phone to Jean's ear.

'Jesus, I need to speak to my sister. It is your will that all be saved. Speak to the medical staff to let Chammy in with the phone so that I can tell Jean to call on your Name. Jean is still alive. There is still life. She can still make a decision for You.'

The Holy Spirit's reminder of God's Word moved me to action.

In John 4:49 Jesus healed a nobleman's child without Jesus being with the child.

'The Spirit of the Lord snatched Philip away' (Acts 8:39).

'The Spirit lifted me up and took me away' (Ezek 3:14).

'Then the Spirit lifted me up into the sky and transported me to Jerusalem in a vision from God' (Ezek 8:3).

My relationship with God was not a 'break the glass in case of emergency' relationship. It was intimate and a daily walk through Jesus Christ and his Word.

I fell to my knees and prayed.

'Jesus, take me to Jean.'

Then I was with Jean and I am sure she heard me pray:

'Jean, call on the name of Jesus. Believe in Him.'

Mark

And now, six months after Jean's death, my spiritual son's drug-filled body was picked up on a pavement in Cape Town. He was barely alive. Twelve years before, this young man had accepted Jesus as his Lord and his Saviour.

Mark was young and Mark was beautiful. Mark was also sad. By the time he had come to live on the Bluff with his aunt when he was 14, life had already punched so many holes into him that whatever kindness he received just leaked out to be lost in the ground.

> '… the devil walks about like a roaring lion, seeking whom he may devour' (1 Pet 5:8, NKJV).

The decision was made to pull the plug on Mark. The life-support machines on this side of life were switched off. It was the other side I was worried about.

One day later Mark was still alive. Two days later, Mark was still alive. Three days later, Mark was still alive.

That roaring lion was pulling at the carpet under my feet. My prayers were flying around in all directions in the spiritual realm. My struggle was varying from giving up to engaging in full-fledged war.

I was angry. I wanted to take this drug-stained Mark and rub him into every youth and shout:

'This is the plan Satan has for you! Have a good look! Take that first drug and see your ending! This will be you lying in your own vomit on a pavement; forgotten. But if you think this ending is bad, you ain't seen nothing yet! After this comes eternal hell. Eternally cut off from God, cursed and thrown into the everlasting fire prepared for the devil and his angels (Matt 25:41). Make your choice today. Choose Jesus. Be hungry for Him. Go, read all about Him. Feed and feed and feed on Jesus so that when you are tempted you can resist the devil and stand; so that if you fall you will get up. Jesus came to give you life in abundance. Don't believe Satan's lies about having fun. Take the step. Put your hand in the hand of Jesus. He gives eternal life. Oh how He loves you!!!!!'

At this time my quiet time reading was in Genesis.

'Is anything too hard for the Lord?' (Gen 18:14).

I prayed:

'Lord, save Mark.'

'... since I have begun, let me speak further to my Lord, even though I am but dust and ashes' (Gen 18:27).

I prayed further:

'Lord, save Mark. I plead with you. He accepted You as Lord when he was 14. Oh Lord, keep that covenant, even though he was unfaithful; show Your mercy. Hear my prayer. I pray in the righteousness of Jesus. Please. Please. Let it be true that my prayer has power. Then I will never stop praying for all my children and people.'

'When Lot still hesitated, the angels seized his hand and the hands of his wife and two daughters and rushed them to safety outside the city, for the Lord was merciful' (Gen 19:16).

I fell down on my face and visited Mark in his coma.

'Mark, this is Aunty Glenda. Do you remember you gave your life to Jesus at the youth group in my home? Mark, call on the name of Jesus. Believe that Jesus is the Son of God and died for your sins.'

The following verses came into my prayer for him:

'Purify me from my sins, and I will be clean; wash me, and I will be whiter than snow. Don't keep looking at my sins. Remove the stain of my guilt' (Ps 51:7,9).

'But God had listened to Abraham's request and kept Lot safe ...' (Gen 19:29).

Mark died.

Next day. Enter 'Doubting Thomas'. I did not need to look in a mirror to see the devil sitting squarely on my left shoulder.

'You weren't really with Mark, you know. You weren't really with Jean, you know. You only think this to make yourself feel better.'

I am so ashamed to admit that I fell into doubt and depression. I was so sad. While with Mark and with Jean, praying for them, it was more real than this moment is; I was at total peace.

Jesus, I am like Thomas, I need to see the nail marks in your hand. I need a sign. I know to Job you gave nothing but to Gideon you did. I put my fleece out.

My friend Eliza is a gift from God on whose shoulder I can always cry and she reassured me that God would reassure me, as He always does.

The next day I was out walking my dog at the boxing club grounds. Suddenly a van drove into the deserted area and came straight towards me. An angry-looking lady got out and placed herself before me.

'We have church here and your dog messes on our grounds.'

My heart was still sobbing and it did not take much for the tears to leave my heart and expose themselves to this then unknown lady, Veronica. I told her about Mark and Jean and my experience.

Veronica knows Jesus. She assured me that they were saved and that Jesus took them home. She told me of a guy who did not know God at all and 'died' when a jellyfish stung him. While this man was in a coma the Holy Spirit converted him because his mother was praying for him. This guy returned to tell the story. She told me to get the DVD called *Dead Man Walking*. While she talked I felt the Holy Spirit lift me and I knew that Jesus was using this woman's words to reassure me. God even used my dog to bring us together.

(By the way, I always walk with a cut-off Coke bottle or a two litre milk bottle and a plastic bag to pick up my dog's poo. Jesus wants us to keep our world clean and to be considerate to others.)

The story does not end there. When I got home, my tenant, Paul, came up to me and told me he had a movie for me. Yes, you guessed it: it was *Dead Man Walking*! It is also called *A Glimpse of Eternity*. What a faithful God we serve. He meets us in our weaknesses. I believe there is another movie starring Sean Penn which is also called *Dead Man Walking*. It is not that movie. This movie is a Christian film by a man named Ian McCormack.

I want you to know that I had not waited for Jean to be on her deathbed before telling her about Jesus. I had never let an opportunity pass without telling her about Jesus. If necessary I made opportunities. Jean had visited me six months before her death and I had again explained to her how we were cut off from God because of our sin and how God gave us Jesus to die for those sins so that we can be reunited with God and have eternal life. All she had to do was to believe what God had done and to embrace Jesus.

I only remember now, that when Jean's son, Shane, committed suicide about ten years ago, that she had put her hand up in the funeral service and had repeated the Sinner's Prayer.

Jean's friend told me that Jean had complained about me trying to convert her but at the same time she had started watching Christian programmes on television and talked about what she was seeing and hearing. The Holy Spirit was putting a thirst and a hunger for Jesus in her. So there I was in the Spirit with my sister Jean sharing Jesus one more time before she left this world for good. God is so good.

Tragedy

He reveals deep and mysterious things and knows what lies hidden in darkness.

– DANIEL 2:22

When you are sixty and the youngest of five sisters, you expect that Jesus could be nearing completion in preparing a place for you and getting ready to fetch one of you. Then, when He came to fetch my second-eldest sister Hermie's only daughter, as well as her granddaughter in one go, you feel the crash, the silence and the darkness.

It happened in the night. It was a car accident near Graaff Reinet on 9 January 2010, two weeks before Hermie's 70th birthday.

It must have been a terrible crash and then a terrible silence and then a terrible darkness. That darkness, cold and silence enfolded itself around all of us sisters.

'The Lord does whatever pleases Him' (Ps 135:6).

'For everything serves Your plans' (Ps 119:91).

'The Lord has made heaven His throne, from there He rules everything' (Ps 103:19).

I don't know what people do, who don't know God.

I can only tell you what happened as I see it. I can never go into Hermie's heart and experience it. All I could do was to cry together with her on the phone.

My letter to my daughter Kimmie captures my first thoughts and prayers.

'Good morning Kimmie

I did not sleep much. I also thought of all the people in the Bible who lost their children. I know Jacob could not be consoled when he was told Joseph was dead. David fell to pieces when Absalom was killed, even though Absalom had tried to kill him. David also would not eat when his baby from Bathsheba was deadly ill. Job lost all his kids in one go. Mary thought she had lost her Son Jesus. I don't know why I am shocked that God let it happen.

My Bible reading today is Leviticus 10. Aaron lost both his sons in one go. Just like Hermie. Aaron was silent. God told him the family could mourn by tearing their clothes and not combing their hair but Aaron was not allowed to mourn as he was anointed. My heart cried for him. The whole of that chapter is so sad. It just goes to show God's absolute holiness.

My first prayer in every one of my diaries is "Let Your Will Be Done" (together with "Let me love You and don't let me leave You"). So this is God's will. All I can do is watch my sister crumple as if acid was poured over her body and soul and I can do nothing to stop it.

I can hope that God will have it in His will that Jesus fetches Hermie soon so that the pain will go away and she can be with the loving God who will explain everything to her (or won't have to because it won't matter then). And she will see her beloved daughter and granddaughter and sister and husband, and all the mourning will turn to laughter and a joy that has not been experienced in this world.

I am on prayer duty in the church today. That is a hard one. For whatever request I will pray: God, you know what you have ordained in this day for this person. I thank You that You are in control and that You know what is best for us to prepare us for Your Kingdom. I will stand back and let Your will be done on earth as it is in heaven.

God said: "I will never leave you nor forsake you."

Jesus said: "I am with you always."

Love you, Kimmie, my child, for now and for eternity. I thank God that you are His child.

Your Mom'

Because we have the same Spirit dwelling in us and comforting us, I could share with Hermie the encouraging sermon that Kimmie heard that morning, which included Romans 8:18, 'Yet what we suffer now is nothing compared to the glory he will reveal to us later.'

Hermie also acknowledged that her church's silent prayer request to hold her up, reached her heart and strengthened her. Seeing God's presence in Hermie was a testimony to others that Christians seem to mourn in a different way. It is because we know that life with Jesus here continues into eternity after the death of the body.

21

Movie offer — 2010

On 21 January 2010 I got a phone call from a film producer. He was from a well-established film company which was recognised for having made some outstanding films. They have offices in Cape Town and in Los Angeles. They wanted to make a film of my life, to be released internationally.

My first reaction was 'NO'. I am a new person now. That dancer you want to tell about does not exist anymore. That life was boring. If I had anything to tell it would be about now and about the excitement of having Jesus in my life.

He asked me to think about it.

Christians don't think about things, they pray about things.

My reading at this time was from Matthew 4:19: 'Come, follow me, and I will show you how to fish for people!'

A few days later I was in the little printer's shop down the road. I often talk to the lady who owns the shop. She knows my need for ink for my printer in spreading the Word.

That day there was another lady there who was also purchasing ink. We started chatting. Her name was Brenda. She said people often called her 'Glenda Kemp' because she works with snakes and goes around to schools to do demonstrations. I smiled and said that sometimes they call me 'Brenda'.

She told me about her son who has trouble at school and I told her the only answer for our children is to pray for them. There is so much power in our prayers. God is so powerful and loves our children more than we do. I did not feel as if anyone was hearing me. I can't remember what she said but in order to make a point I told how God had protected me in my dancing days even when I was unfaithful to Him. Both ladies went quiet and looked at me — 'What dancing days?'

I had always assumed that the shop owner knew that I was Glenda Kemp. The reaction I got from these two ladies amazed me. Suddenly, they listened to every word I had to say. They were totally with me. I managed to explain my favourite explanation of the Gospel using two rulers to show how we were cut off from God and how Jesus' death on the cross brought us back to God. I could tell all about Jesus and they listened. I explained to them how to give their lives to Jesus and to make Him King of their lives.

This was the event that God used to tell me that I had to say 'Yes' to the movie of my life. The film would give me a new platform to witness for Him.

I find that when I witness to Christians they don't listen because of who I was. When I witness to the world it listens because of who I was.

I discussed it with my husband and told him why I felt I should do it and he agreed.

Eliza and I prayed together. When I sit and pray with Eliza, I feel as if all the giants are so small and I am so strong in Jesus that nothing scares me.

Deuteronomy 1:21 says 'Look! He has placed the land in front of you. Go and occupy it as the Lord, the God of your ancestors has promised you. Don't be afraid. Don't be discouraged.' A little further on in Deuteronomy 1:30 it goes on to say 'The Lord your God is going ahead of you.'

I had long discussions with God. What if the movie turned out to be a porno movie? God told me that I was not to be concerned about what people thought of me. If anyone had a problem with believing who I am now, then they had a problem with Jesus. Jesus died for my sins and for everyone else's sins. He is in the renewing business and I was living proof of what He could do with a life. Whoever did not believe what He did for me would have to look at their relationship with Jesus and work on more intimacy with Him. I was to hand everything over to Him and to trust and obey.

I also discussed it with my ministers at the Bluff Methodist Church. They know who I am in Christ and they gave me their blessing on the project. We prayed that God will be glorified and that his will would be done.

The producer called again and I agreed to give his film company permission to make the movie. We set a date for 9 February 2010 for him and his 'crew' to come from Cape Town to interview me in Durban.

The film crew had done their homework. They had dug up things I knew about and other things I had forgotten about. It was traumatic having to go back into a past which Jesus had removed as far from me as the East is from the West. With the knowledge of Him having a plan for my life I obediently exposed the truth as it was for me and as I see it now. I know now why it is so important for me to constantly fill myself with the Word.

'And you must commit yourselves wholeheartedly to these commands that I am giving you today. Repeat them again and again to your children. Talk about them when you are at home and when you are on the road, when you arc going to bed and when you are getting up. Tie them to your hands and wear them on your forehead as reminders. Write them on the doorposts of your house and on your gates' (Deut 6:6–9).

Why, this is what I did with the worldly things. For 44 years I filled myself with all the world has to offer. The results were 'My people are being destroyed because they don't know me' (Hosea 4:6).

The producer asked me how I would feel about a famous South African actress playing the role of Glenda. I went quiet. I really wanted a Christian person to play the part. He told me she would be ideal as she could imitate my accent and was so excellent at portraying people. Of course it would have to be a very good script in order to get her. I now wonder how I could have hesitated about her playing the part. Everyone else thought it would be the best thing that could ever happen.

Two weeks later I was made an offer. I was totally lost. I took the offer to God and asked Him to provide someone to advise me. I had no idea what was the right thing to do. I knew I needed help from Christians who had walked the 'movie' path before.

The following is an email I sent to a well-known South African evangelist:

Dear Xxxxx

Greetings in the name of our Lord Jesus.

My name is Glenda Harper. I was Glenda Kemp, the stripper. Was.

A film company with offices in Cape Town and Los Angeles has contacted me to turn my life story into an international film. My first answer was a definite 'no' as Glenda Kemp died with Christ and I am a new person. That life was boring and wasted. Then God spoke clearly to me through something that happened and through his Word, that I have to have the movie done. This would give new platforms for Jesus to speak and work through me. My reason for living is Christ. For seventeen years I have been in the Word and the Word in me. Two people who currently work for you have been part of my spiritual walk and have informed me that you are willing to talk with me. I seek Godly advice as I have no idea what contract to have drawn up.

Your sincere sister in Christ.

Glenda Harper

I received no reply. I wrote again and asked just for an acknowledgment that this man had received the letter. I then tried phoning and was told on calling their number a second time that my letter was there and that it would be put with the priority mail.

I never heard from them.

I phoned *Joy* magazine who put me onto Christian lawyers but I could not afford them.

I was at a dead end as far as advice was concerned. I handed it over to God and prayed that whatever decision I made would be in his will.

I am constantly approached by magazines and newspapers to comment on topics or to inform their readers about my present life. I have never asked for a cent as every article is an opportunity for me to witness. With the movie it was different; I made it clear to the producer that I would want a fee for the rights to make a movie about my life. Eliza and I have our ministry of distributing Bibles and printing sections of the Bible with prayers accompanying them. The finances from the movie would boost the spreading of the gospel.

The movie company made me an offer.

Then a very ugly thing happened to me. The old nature reared its ugly head and I wrote an almost 'rude' letter to the producer in which I demanded much more than what they were offering.

The company offered me twice the original amount and sent me the contract. To have signed that contract would have been like Esau signing away his birth rights in Genesis. I would have no right over any part of my life ever again.

God clearly reminded me in my reading at the time not to forget my reason for having given the go-ahead for the movie.

'Stay on the path that the Lord your God has commanded you to follow' (Deut 5:33).

'But that is the time to be careful! Beware that in your plenty you do not forget the Lord your God and disobey his commands, regulations and decrees that I am giving you today' (Deut 8:11).

'... do not fall into the trap of following their customs and worshiping their gods' (Deut 12:30).

I realized I had been influenced by worldly comments about how much money I would be making.

I phoned the producer and asked him if we could restart negotiations from the beginning. I only wanted to give them the rights to make the movie of my life and after three years the rights should expire. This would not include all rights to my life. The money was not important.

A new agreement was drawn up. I signed it.

I think it was at this point that the desire was born to write a book about Jesus in the life of Glenda Kemp. I felt like the woman at the well. My encounter with Jesus wanted me to testify 'Come see a Man who told me all things that I ever did' (John 4:29, NKJV), and my prayer was: 'And many of the Samaritans of that city believed in Him because of the word of the woman who testified' (John 4:39, NKJV).

God showed me clearly in his Word what he wanted this book to represent.

'Make a replica of a poisonous snake and attach it to a pole. All who are bitten will live if they simply look at it!' (Num 21:8).

It is God's mercy in full power over me that speaks of a love that takes that which poisons and changes it into that which will live.

'... pray to the Lord that He takes away the serpents from us' (Num 21:7).

'And as Moses lifted up the serpent in the wilderness, even so must the Son of Man be lifted up; that whoever believes in Him should not perish but have eternal life. For God so loved the world that He gave His only begotten Son, that whoever believes in Him should not perish but have everlasting life. For God did not send His Son into the world to condemn the world, but that the world through Him might be saved' (John 3:14–17, NKJV).

There is now no condemnation for me!!! Praise the Lord!

Joan

It was four days before the interview with Mendy that my sister Joan was admitted into hospital. Her migraines were unbearable and doctors were now testing her for meningitis. We had thought her illness was the result of stress from the loss of Hermie's child and grandchild who were also very near to Joan.

Then the most wonderful thing happened. On the night of 5 February 2010 Joan phoned me from the hospital and told me her sins were lying so heavily on her that she could not get peace about them. She wanted to know Jesus as her saviour. We prayed and Joanie my beloved sister became reborn as Jesus tells us to do in John 3. She phoned me back half an hour later to tell me that she now felt so unbelievably light even though her body was tired beyond description. That night she had two strokes and went into a coma.

On 10 February I received a phone call from my sister's doctor to say we should come as Joan was dying.

The faithful, understanding God I serve even gave me the words in my daily reading to express my pain and anger towards Him.

'... the load is far too heavy! If this is how you intend to treat me, just go ahead and kill me. Do me a favour and spare me this misery!' (Num 11:14–15).

And then this mighty, merciful God spoke to me as clearly as a daddy sitting in the room with me.

'Has my arm lost its power? Now you will see whether or not my word comes true!' (Num 11:23).

And God did show me.

God showed me darkness. God showed me light. God showed me Jesus.

My sister in ICU had swollen to an unrecognizable mass. I stroked a spot I found where no life-giving pipes intruded. I stroked her spirit. My sister in birth and my sister in Christ. Truly sisters. We sat together with Jesus. I sang praises and prayed that God be glorified.

A very sombre family gathered in my sister's lounge to meet with one of her doctor friends. We were informed that the tests revealed that Joanie had severe brain damage. Should she live (which was most unlikely), she would never be the same Joanie we knew. She would need to be institutionalized, be unable to speak and would not recognize any of us.

I then shared with everyone about the phone call made to me in which she accepted Jesus as her saviour. I rejoiced that she was a citizen of heaven no matter what happened.

The doctor, who knew my sister well, was offended. 'Joan is the most generous person I have ever met. She would go to heaven anyway!'

I reminded the doctor, and the whole family gathered there, that the Bible says our good deeds are like filthy rags to the Lord. We are all sinners. Jesus said in John 14:6, 'I am the way, the truth, and the life. No one comes to the Father except through Me.' It is only because of believing and accepting Jesus as Lord, that Joanie (or any of us) will going to heaven; not because of any good deed we had done. Jesus died to wipe out our sins so that we can be reconciled to God.

My words were not well-received in that gathering. I went and lay on my bed where I curled up in a foetal position and told Jesus 'It's all about you Jesus. It is not about me.'

I then heard someone softly calling my name. It was my sister's daughter. She wanted to give her life to Jesus. Oh the things God showed me!

A funeral was being planned.

More than a week passed and no funeral was held. The doctor would not switch off the life-support machines.

We sisters and the rest of the family returned home.

This is the news reported to me two weeks later.

Joanie's specialist doctor was busy doing something around the 'woman' in a coma when he heard someone saying, 'Good morning Dr Le Roux.' I don't know what Dr Le Roux said then, but I am sure there must have been a silence. Joanie said it again. My sister lives!

Glenda and Joan after her illness

Soon after Joanie left ICU I flew back to Johannesburg to be at her side. Every morning my brother-in-law, Koos, dropped me at her hospital bedside and every evening he fetched me. I would read God's Word to Joanie, play praise and worship songs and massage her body. In that week I saw her master talking, walking, eating and using a toilet all by herself. The rhythm to which she fought for every slow, hard-won victory was 'Praise the Lord'.

Joan tells that while she was in that coma, God appeared to her. He had put all her sins on a table. Then He had taken his arm and swept them all off. She was left without any sins.

Joan, Glenda, Linda and Hermie – Christmas 2010

'Oh, give thanks to the Lord!

Call upon His name,

Make known His deeds among the peoples!

Sing to Him, sing Psalms to Him;

Talk of all His wondrous works!

Glory in His holy name.

Let the heart of those rejoice who seek the Lord!

Seek the Lord and His strength;

Seek His face evermore!

Remember His marvelous works

which He has done.'

Psalm 105:1–5, NKJV

Glenda Kemp - Snake Dancer

22

The never-ending story

In the June 2010 issue of *Joy* magazine there is a news item on page 13 which reads: 'International *Naked News* to come to SA.' Directly underneath it is an article headed 'Boycott *Naked News* Channel', in which we are called upon to stop this from happening. Interestingly, if we were asked to form a barricade against these ladies, there is a good chance that I would be one of the 'religious women' forming part of the barricade.

You never know which side you will be on! Because of where I come from I know that there is a much deeper root to follow, which involves naming the people involved one by one before God, praying that they may meet Jesus and that they may put Him on the throne of their lives. It involves interceding for those who do not know … that the truth might set them free … that they will experience the love of a God who sent his Son to die for them. Such a privilege to know the power of prayer.

This verse took on a whole new meaning for me today:

'… while we do not look at the things which are seen, but at the things which are not seen. For the things which are seen are temporary, but the things which are not seen are eternal' (2 Cor 4:18, NKJV).

The only photos you will find in my home are the few stuck up with 'Prestik' on the door of my linen cupboard. Words of life will smile at you from various places on my kitchen and lounge walls. If I should fail to praise God, then my walls will. It never occurred to me that this was unusual until a family friend informed me that my sisters thought I was a bit over the top.

The point I want to make is that looking at the photographs on the door showed me how the things my eyes see have all been subject to change. Those things that were, are no more; and those that are, are not the same. But the words on my walls are eternal. They will never change.

'Heaven and earth will disappear, but My words will never disappear' (Matt 24:35).

'I give them eternal life, and they will never perish' (John 10:28).

'For we know that if our earthly house, this tent, is destroyed, we have a building from God, a house not made with hands; eternal in the heavens' (2 Cor 5:10).

There is one thing I will never understand. Why do so many Christians not read the Word of God? Why do so many Christians base their quiet time on a devotional book that has one verse from God and a full page of human opinion? Surely every Christian should make an appointment and covenant with God to read one book of the Bible every day until they have read through the entire Bible from beginning to end? How come the same verses do the Christian rounds and no one knows what comes before or after that verse?

A Christian friend was handing out a lovely verse at Bible Study which reads: 'May the Lord watch between you and me when we are absent from each other' (Genesis 31:49).

The request for God to watch 'between you and me' was in fact so that Jacob and Laban would not pass a certain point and be able to harm each other. It was a boundary line drawn between them. No one in the Bible Study knew what came before and after the verse.

'Jesus replied: "Your mistake is that you don't know the Scriptures, and you don't know the power of God"' (Matt 22:29).

'If you abide in My word, you are My disciples indeed. And you shall know the truth, and the truth shall make you free' (John 8:31–32).

After one of Angus Buchan's *Mighty Men Conference* meetings I spoke to men who were overjoyed at the Spirit-filled messages and wonderful things that had happened over the weekend. When I asked if they were now making time to read God's Word undiluted, their answer was 'No'. But that was what the entire message had been about! Everyone is too busy. Give up your TV time! Use the time you use to read a newspaper or a magazine!

It was in order to get this message across to my youth group that I wrote the play about the husband who marries his lovely bride and then seals her mouth with sticky tape and locks her up in the cupboard while enjoying his life of freedom as a single man. Come Sunday, time to visit the parents, he takes the bride out of the cupboard and apologizes to her while telling her how beautiful she is and how he adores her. Once back home after parading her to the world, he locks her back in the cupboard. Jesus wants us to be in a personal relationship with Him on a daily basis. 'And you must love the Lord your God with all your heart, all your soul, all your mind, and all your strength' (Mark 12:30).

'… Whoever drinks of the water that I shall give him will never thirst. But the water that I shall give him will become in him a fountain of water springing up into everlasting life' (John 4:14, NKJV).

This is my life story. You also have a life story.

In 1 Corinthians 3:13, we read 'But on the judgment day, fire will reveal what kind of work each builder has done. The fire will show if a person's work has any value.'

Yes, my life and yours could lie between the two covers of a book. But just how thick will that book be on Judgement Day? Horror of horrors — what if the pages are blank and we find ourselves on the worst side of Revelation's happenings? Luke 10:20 says, ' … rejoice because your names are registered in

heaven', and in Revelation 20:15 it states, 'And anyone whose name was not found recorded in the Book of Life was thrown into the lake of fire.'

In a newspaper article written during the 70s, Glenda Kemp was referred to as the 'scarlet woman' of South Africa's entertainment world.

What does God say about that?

'"Come now, and let us reason together,"

Says the Lord,

"Though your sins are like scarlet,

They shall be as white as snow;

Though they are red like crimson

They shall be as wool"' (Isa 1:18, NKJV).

How wonderful to be able to say for sure that I am a new creation in Christ. All the old things have passed away. This is a new day. Come Lord Jesus, come!

23

A visit to London in 2011

Soho — the sexpots of London

In September 2011 I found myself back in London to attend Kimmie's graduation as a Speech Therapist. What a wonderful ceremony and how I enjoyed seeing my child fulfil her dream to be qualified in the work she loves. I took the opportunity to revisit some of the places I knew from my days as a stripper in London.

Should the story of this visit start in sleazy Soho, or in an old lady's dreams?

Let's start with Soho — the sex pots of London.

Thirty years ago I walked here. Today, 30 September 2011, I walk here, big-eyed in remembering.

Now the dream part. Ever have a recurring dream, year in and year out? Well I do.

Place: Soho.

Venue: Strip joint (that never was) next to a stage door (that was).

Let me explain — I worked in a strip club called Paul Raymond's Revue bar. Our stage door was way removed from the theatre. Next to the stage door there was just a wall to go past to get to the theatre around the corner.

Now tell this to my dream and it insists there is a club next door to the stage door, and that there in that club (which never existed) is where I have to appear on stage, wearing clothes for the sole purpose of removing them in front of an audience. Now we reach the nightmare part of the dream ....

I am not ready. The drums are rolling my announcement. My showbiz clothes are scrambled in a suitcase and what I do pull out is full of holes. To crown the nightmare, I am not 26 but 62. Help!

Ready or not, here I come. If your name is called out you go. I walk sheepishly on to the stage. A silence. Surprise element? Then it happens: I tell them about Jesus! The love of Jesus strips the occupants of the club of all that is preventing Jesus from occupying the limelight. The darkness becomes light. Jesus is centre stage. The Holy Spirit is bringing the past into his presence.

Back to Soho 2011

Jojo's transvestite ladies

Piccadilly Circus remembered me.

Brewer Street remembered me.

St James' Residence building in Brewer Street remembered me.

The café across the road remembered me.

But Paul Raymond's Revue Bar did not remember me.

I was just in time to witness its death. The big neon lights were still there but its shine was off. The billboard being in the process of being removed, was evidence of my past being taken away. I almost ran to the once-elaborate entrance hall where I expected to see my nude pictures displayed. There I found two men moving big boxes amongst undone surroundings.

'Is this ... was this Raymond's Revue Bar theatre?' I asked.

'Yes it was,' they replied.

'Heaven and earth will disappear, but My words will never disappear' (Matt 24:35).

'The grass withers and the flowers fall; but the word of our God stands forever' (Isa 40:8).

I stand before the stage door. That hole in the wall that let me in and let me out. It is still there. It remembered me.

Then … next to the stage door … yes, you guessed it … the club in my dreams. Every bit, exactly as in my dreams. Now it had a name and real people working inside. 'Jojo's' is its name — and the names of the people inside? Jesus knows every name and he knew every person even before they were born. If it took an old lady's dream to tell them He loves them then that is what it will take. The power of prayer. I pray for you, Jojo's beautiful people.

I was so dumbstruck that I could tell Kimmie only the next morning, after having clutched my Bible to my heart throughout the night, wanting to squeeze the imprint of God's will onto my day. It was my last day in London. Time was up. I had visited my dream and had done nothing about it!

Kim and Glenda at Kim's graduation in London

From here on I can truly say that I had nothing to do with the events that followed.

'Kimmie, I must go back to the club!'

I had a sense of urgency as I went through my Emergency 911 kit; my travelling companion. I felt I had to go back to the club. I packed two small booklets with lifesaving verses and two salvation tracts that tell how to live eternally with the One who loves you more than any person can ever love you. On one salvation pamphlet I wrote:

> *Dear Ladies*
>
> *I once was in my twenties and worked here around the corner. Today I am 62 and visiting the past. You are the future. Please visit me on my blog http://glendakemp.wordpress.com*
>
> *I would love to get to know you.*

So there I was standing in front of Jojo's, armed with God's Word; booklets small enough to slide through a slit in the door but big enough to love its occupants all the way in to a new creation with God forever.

> *My personal message to you, Soho, is not about what is wrong or what is right or who is what and why and when. My challenge to you is this: 'Go and read the Bible.' Take two years to read through the entire Bible. Start with the book of John in the New Testament. Pull a chair out and ask Jesus to sit on it while you read and read and talk to Him. Read through the New Testament first. Then read the New Testament again while adding Old Testament books with it. Read the book of 1 John over and over. The ideal situation is if you and a friend start doing it at the same time (in your own individual quiet time). Then get together and discuss what you have read.*
>
> *I am not saying for one moment that you should change anything in your life; all I am asking is that you read the Bible. God speaks today just as He did then.*
>
> *God bless you.*

'And we know that God causes everything to work together for the good of those who love God and are called according to his purpose for them.'

Romans 8:28

24

So just what happened to the movie offer?

What I once saw on one of my walks on the beach made my mouth hang open and then, instinctively, made me run for my life. It appeared like the white vapour trail a jet plane leaves behind in the sky. But this jet was heading down toward the ocean.

What this 'jet' did to the water when it hit it like a bomb was shocking. The water gaped open and climbed into the air to allow the force to take over. There was a hole in the ocean and the hole was moving towards the land. By now I knew that it was no jet; it was a tornado and it was heading towards me and my life — ready to make a hole and send things flying.

Before I reached my car it was gone, not even leaving a scar on the ocean.

That is how the movie offer came into my life. I was minding my own business walking on the beach. It made a hole in my life and flung up details I had forgotten about like flying debris. I called on God to pin it into order and then suddenly the movie was gone — not a sign, not a word, and there I was standing with a book.

What is the difference between the tornado and the movie? The tornado is not recorded; no scar, no picture. As for the movie, there was a signed contract, sealed and delivered; correspondence, gifts and information that the script was near completion. After forwarding my unedited book to the film company there was a long silence and much later an email to say that there were problems and that the script had lost its writer — due to unforeseen circumstances.

However, at the time of writing, it seems that a new scriptwriter has been found and that the movie may soon be on track again.

God says all things work together for good for those who love Him. Who knows? The results of all this excitement? I give you my story, and may God bless you with it.

Appendix A — Pamphlets

Eliza and I handed these pamphlets out with our Bibles. We based the first page of the pamphlet on the *Billy Graham Christian Worker's Handbook*.

STEPS TO PEACE WITH GOD

1. God's Plan—Peace and Life

God loves you and wants you to experience His peace and life.

The BIBLE says: "For God so loved the world that He gave His only begotten Son, that whoever believes in Him should not perish but have everlasting life" (John 3:16).

2. Our Problem—Separation

Being at peace with God is not automatic, because by nature you are separated from God.

The BIBLE says: "For all have sinned and fall short of the glory of God" (Romans 3:23).

3. God's Remedy—The Cross

God's love bridges the gap of separation between God and you. When Jesus Christ died on the cross and rose from the grave, He paid the penalty for your sins.

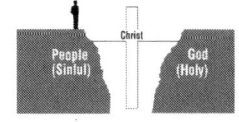

The BIBLE says: "He personally carried the load of our sins in his own body when he died on the cross" (1 Peter 2:24, TLB).

4. Our Response—Receive Christ

You cross the bridge into God's family when you receive Christ by personal invitation.

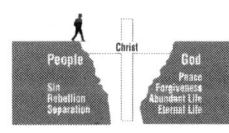

The BIBLE says: "But as many as received Him, to them He gave the right to become children of God, even to those who believe in His name" (John 1:12).

To receive Christ you need to do four things:

1. ADMIT your spiritual need. "I am a sinner."

2. REPENT and be willing to turn from your sin.

3. BELIEVE that Jesus Christ died for you on the cross.

4. RECEIVE, through prayer, Jesus Christ into your heart and life.

CHRIST says, "Behold, I stand at the door and knock. If anyone hears My voice and opens the door, I will come in" (Revelation 3:20).

The BIBLE says, "Whoever calls upon the name of the Lord will be saved" (Romans 10:13).

What to Pray:

Dear Lord Jesus, I know that I am a sinner and need Your forgiveness. I believe that You died for my sins. I want to turn from my sins. I now invite You to come into my heart and life. I want to trust and follow You as Lord and Savior. In Jesus' name, Amen.

Questions and Answers

On the other side of the tract we reprinted extracts from *Joy* magazine — www.joymag.co.za — *'Biblically-based answers by Val Waldeck'*.

Question: Do Christians believe every word of the Bible? Or do they believe that it is full of error?

Answer: Yes, they do believe every word! So did Jesus. He declared in John 17:17 *'Your Word is Truth'*. He did not say it contained Truth together with error — it is Truth and, therefore, wholly to be believed and trusted. He told some folk who were arguing about the resurrection, that they were completely off track *'not knowing the Scriptures'* (Matt 22:29).

2 Timothy 3:16 declares that *'all Scripture'* is inspired by God Himself and Holy men of old spoke (and wrote) as *'they were moved by the Holy Spirit'* (2 Peter 1:21). The Holy Spirit, who inspired the Word, must be depended upon to interpret that Word because the Bible does contain some things that are difficult to understand (2 Peter 1:20). Unstable people love to force Scripture to fit their personal opinions (2 Peter 3:16). The secret to true fulfilment lies in the Word (Psalm 1:1–3).

* * * * *

Question: How do we know that there is a God?

Answer: One way is to look at creation. The book of Romans in the New Testament tells us that God has put his knowledge in our hearts. *'Since earliest times men have seen the earth and sky and all God made, and have known of his existence and great eternal power. So they will have no excuse (when they stand before God at Judgment Day)'* (Romans 1:19,20). The watch on your arm didn't 'just happen'. Someone carefully designed it and put it together. And it is the same with the world. Everything you see around you shouts loudly that the Great Designer and Creator made it all perfectly. Another way to be sure is to ask Him! God is personal and He can communicate with you. The testimony of thousands of his children (from Bible times right up to today) is that He definitely talks to them. Why not start by reading his written revelation of Himself — the

Bible? Start with the New Testament and humbly ask the Lord Jesus Christ to meet with you. That will be the most exciting thing you have ever done!

* * * * *

Question: Surely we all believe in the same God but call Him different names?

Answer: Jesus said: *'I am the Way, the Truth and the life; No one comes to the Father except through Me'* (John 14:6). Either He was deluded, or a deceiver, or He meant what He said — there is only one God and one way to the Father. If there were another way to Heaven, the death and resurrection of Christ would be superfluous and unnecessary.

Our God is not schizophrenic — using different names to propagate different belief systems. His Word is: *'For there is only one God and one Mediator who can reconcile God and people ... Christ Jesus. He gave his life to purchase freedom for everyone. This is the message that God gave to the world at the proper time'* (1 Timothy 2:6). In Noah's day, the Ark was the only means of salvation. Christ is God's Ark for 'whosoever' will believe, regardless of their faith or creed.

* * * * * * *

Glenda Kemp - Snake Dancer

Appendix B — Glossary

braai – barbecue

Click Song – Real name *Qongqothwane*, is a traditional song of the Xhosa people of South Africa. It is sung at weddings to bring good fortune

Cook and Enjoy for Beginners – The English version of the well-known Afrikaans cookbook *Kook en Geniet*

Dagwood – A huge sandwich with many layers of filling

Ek is 'n dapper muis – A children's song. In English it is *I'm a brave, brave mouse*. The mouse says he is not afraid of anything but in fact he is

frikkadels – meat balls

Haas Das – A rabbit puppet who read the 'news' on a children's TV programme

heerlike – wonderful, delicious (adj.)

Huisgenoot – Much-loved Afrikaans family-focused magazine

Ipi Tombi – (IsiZulu) Literally: 'Where is the girl?' A South African musical (1974) which enjoyed international success

Joy – A South African Christian magazine

Keur – Afrikaans magazine featuring news and gossip of film stars

leguaan – Monitor lizard. From the Dutch 'iguana'

Matric – Public examination written in Grade 12, the final year of school

mealie – maize, corn

Oom – Uncle (respectful term for any adult male, not necessarily a relation)

Oupa – Grandpa

SARS – South African Revenue Services, formerly the Receiver of Revenue

Scope – English-language magazine featuring scandalous stories

sokkies – dances/discos

stompie – cigarette butt

Tannie – Aunty (respectful term for any adult woman, not necessarily a relation)

tjorrie – old car

TLC – Tender Loving Care

Uiltjie – A nickname meaning 'Little Owl'

vetkoek – Literally 'fat cake'. Traditional Afrikaner pastry. It is dough deep-fried in cooking oil and often filled with cooked mince.

Voortrekker kappie – Bonnet with a large brim worn by the early Afrikaner women

* * * * * * *

Appendix C — Glenda's Family Tree

Generation No. 1

1. MARTHA[1] GROENEWALD was born 28 April 1917, and died 4 May 2005. Married (1) DIRK CORNELIUS KEMP. Married (2) VIC CLOETE.

Children of MARTHA GROENEWALD and DIRK KEMP are:

      i.   **LINDA**[2] KEMP, b. 30 October 1937; m. (1) KOBUS KRIEL. They had 3 children. Married (2) JAMES VAN ROOYEN.

      ii.   **HERMIE** KEMP, b. 28 January 1940; m. ANTON VAN ZUYLEN. They had 3 children. Anton died June 2007. Hermie lost her daughter and granddaughter in a car accident in January 2010.

      iii.   **JEAN** KEMP, b. 18 September 1941; d. 22 July 2009; m. RONALD STRICKLAND. They had 2 children. Jean divorced but never remarried.

      iv.   **DIRK** CORNELIUS KEMP, b. 5 January 1943; d. 1987; m. (1) GERTA AUSTIN. They had 2 children. He married (2) JOYCE. Gerta remarried GIDEON LUBBE.

      v.   **JOAN** KEMP, b. 16 July 1946; m. KOOS WEST. They had 3 children. Koos died 2011.

2.   vi.   **GLENDA** KEMP, b. 13 May 1949.

Child of MARTHA GROENEWALD and VIC CLOETE is:

      vii.   **DALE**[2] CLOETE, b. 4 June 1957; m. SONJA VAN HEERDEN. No children.

Generation No. 2

2.   GLENDA[2] KEMP was born 13 May 1949. Married (1) KARL KOCZWARA. Married (2) PETER HARPER.

Child of GLENDA KEMP and KARL KOCZWARA is:

      i.   **KIM**[3] KOCZWARA, b. 7 December 1982.

* * * * * * *

Made in the USA
Coppell, TX
04 November 2020